LOVE'S $WEET RETURN

LOVE'S $WEET RETURN

THE HARLEQUIN STORY

Margaret Ann Jensen

Bowling Green State University Popular Press
Bowling Green, Ohio 43403

Library of Congress Catalogue Card No.: 84-72407
ISBN: 0-87972-318-1 Clothbound

First published by:
The Women's Educational Press
16 Baldwin Street
Toronto, Ontario, Canada

To my grandmother, Mary Schultz,
who, by her example, taught me about
the strength, warmth and creativity of
"ordinary women."

CONTENTS

ACKNOWLEDGMENTS

The myth of individual authorship becomes apparent when one sits down at the end of the writing process to acknowledge one's debts. *Love's $weet Return* is the outgrowth of a doctoral dissertation I completed at McMaster University in Hamilton, Ontario. One of the most rewarding aspects of graduate school was the intellectual and emotional companionship shared by the students. Ann Duffy, Marie Boutilier, Linda Gardner, Rona Achilles, Mary Jane Price and Teri Spinola have continued to provide that support over the years. My "bookstore friends" – Marilyn Elkin and John Barker – have also been a continuous source of encouragement and hospitality for which I am grateful.

Similarly, at Hamline University in St. Paul, Minnesota, my colleagues have offered advice, insights and necessary distractions. Diane Clayton, Martin Markowitz, Kim Guenther, Beth Gunderson, Carol Johansen and Quay Grigg – thank you. Emily Gurnon capably assisted me with library research and Bruce Johansen acted as "a sounding board" for most of my ideas. His good humour, intelligence and enthusiasm are deeply appreciated. I am indebted to Carole Brown, with whom I have co-taught on two occasions. I have learned a great deal from her analysis of the texts we studied; her knowledge has enriched my understanding of literature.

My family patiently accepted my absences when my work kept me away from home. The support of my parents – Melvin and Freda Jensen – has been especially important. My father is "a reader" and it is to him that I owe my interest in formula fiction.

The Ontario Arts Council, The Hanna Foundation and Hamline University have given me financial support that facilitated my research. Women's Press has been extremely helpful as well. I would like to particularly thank Jane Springer for her editorial skill, flexibility, ability to ask crucial questions and hard work. I have enjoyed working with her and her contributions have immeasureably strengthened my analysis. Thanks also to Judy McClard and Daphne Read, who guided me through the early stages of the book, and to the Women's Press staff: Liz Martin, Sharon Nelson, Lois Pike and Margie Wolfe.

All of these people and organizations, in addition to the women readers who kindly consented to be interviewed, have enabled me to work and have affected my thinking on romances. This book would not have been possible without their assistance.

— M. J.

THE SOCIAL SIGNIFICANCE OF HARLEQUIN ROMANCES

> Come into the world of Harlequin novels ... and be a part of a wonderful dream.... Read one ... and discover our world. It's a beautiful place to be. *You belong in the world of Harlequin.*
>
> Harlequin advertisement

> If placed end to end, Harlequin books sold in 1981 could run along both sides of the Nile, both sides of the Amazon, and one side of the Rio Grande. If all the words of all the Harlequin books sold in 1981 were laid end to end, they would stretch 1000 times around the earth and 93 times to the moon.
>
> Harlequin publicity release

"It is indeed highly significant that ..." Unfortunately at this point in his essay's opening sentence, Duncan, an English graduate student in Margaret Atwood's *The Edible Woman,* gets stuck and can write no more. One sympathizes. Few issues are so clear-cut that they can live up to such a confident beginning. In spite of the momentary setback, Duncan and his colleagues push on, creating in the process significance where none existed and where some would say none is warranted. A study of Harlequin romances might fall into the latter category in many people's judgment. These people, however, are probably unaware of the pervasive popularity of romances. *Publishers Weekly* estimates that there are over twenty million readers in the United States alone who will buy an estimated half-billion dollars' worth of romances yearly.[1] Harlequins themselves account for an even bigger share of the paperback market in Canada (28 percent of all paperbacks sold) than in the United States (10 to 12 percent of all paperbacks sold).[2] Furthermore, with speed and success that defy cultural differences, Harlequin Enterprises has expanded its operations beyond the English-speaking world to publish its novels in twelve languages that sell in ninety-eight countries around the world. The sun never sets on Harlequin romances!

Although romances are big business and big news, until recently the halls of academe have not been interested in looking at such "trash" or any other form of popular culture except to condemn them for pandering to the "low-brow" tastes of the masses. "Harlequin Romances are all alike," scholars point out. "They're trite and badly written – pure purple prose. Don't waste your time reading them." Harlequins are indeed "all alike" in that they are formula fiction, but the other pejorative comments indicate a basic misunderstanding of the nature and purpose of popular culture.

John Cawelti, professor of English and humanities and author of *Adventure, Mystery, and Romance,* argues that formula fiction is characterized by two main features: it is a highly standardized repetitious literature and its primary purpose is reassuring escape and entertainment.[3] These two traits distinguish it from "serious" literature, which Cawelti prefers to call "mimetic" literature (that is, reproductive of reality) to avoid the value connotations implicit in the term "serious" and others like "high-brow" and "low-brow." In contrast to formula fiction, mimetic fiction is valued for its originality and ability to enlighten the reader. Cawelti points out that most literature contains elements of both types but clearly some literature more closely approximates mimetic fiction while other is best classified as formula fiction.

The characters in formula fiction are usually rather simple sketches or even caricatures, while characters in mimetic fiction are frequently complex and ambiguous. In addition, the artistic challenge to the writer of mimetic literature is different from the challenge to the writer of formula fiction who must, instead of creating new characters and ideas, revitalize old stereotypes without adding anything drastically new. Even the intent, process and result of reading these two types of fiction are distinct. The reader of mimetic fiction is usually forced to examine her or his life, attitudes and behaviour but there is no such necessary comparison between fiction and reality for the reader of formula fiction.[4] If she or he makes any comparisons, it is likely to be between different examples of the same type of formula fiction. A romance reader may compare gothics to contemporary romances or Janet Dailey to Violet Winspear but these comparisons are within the genre of romantic fiction.

This split between the two types of fiction is paralleled by a split in the ranks of readers and critics. On the one side are those who never read anything but mimetic fiction and feel that all literature should be original and purposeful. They believe that a reader should "get something" out of a book, should be affected by it either emotionally or intellectually. They measure formula fiction with mimetic standards and find it wanting. On the other side are those people who never read anything but formula fiction and feel that mimetic literature is too "heavy," depressing and obtuse. The mimetic readers have academic credentials on their side and theirs has been the dominant voice but they are outnumbered by formula fiction readers.

Yet comparing mimetic and formula fiction is like comparing apples and oranges. No one is any the wiser for saying that apples are inferior oranges. Similarly, we must not automatically dismiss formula fiction as a degraded form of mimetic fiction:

> The trouble with this sort of approach is that it tends to make us perceive and evaluate formula literature simply as an inferior or perverted form of something better, instead of seeing its "escapist" characteristics as aspects of an artistic type with its own purposes and justifications. After all, while most of us would condemn escapism as a total way of life, our capacity to use our imaginations to construct alternative worlds into which we can temporarily retreat is certainly a central human characteristic and seems, on the whole, a valuable one.[5]

Cawelti suggests that classifying formula fiction as a game or a form of extended solitary play might remove the objection that formula fiction is not really "literature" and also explain the fascination of continual repetition, which is incomprehensible to someone who values the uniqueness of mimetic literature:

> Like such games as football or baseball, formula stories are individual versions of a general pattern defined by a set of rules. While the rules remain the same, the highly varied ways in which they can be embodied in particular characters and actions produce a patterned experience of excitement, suspense, and release that, in the case of the great games, can be perennially engrossing no matter how often the game is repeated.[6]

Repetitive games and stories appeal to two conflicting psychological needs, according to Cawelti. We need excitement to escape the boredom that pervades our everyday lives but we also need security to protect us from our anxieties about life's uncertainties and tragedies. Escapist entertainment temporarily resolves the tension between these conflicting needs by emphasizing danger, sex and violence within the context of a tightly controlled fictional structure. As a result, our basic sense of security and order is intensified rather than disrupted ... ' "

Cawelti's insights into the distinctive characteristics, appeal and viability of formula fiction inform my analysis of Harlequin Enterprises, romances and readers. The interconnection between women's social realities and romances is the primary focus of this book. The influx of women into the labour force, the "sexual revolution" and the women's movement have all substantially altered women's lives since the end of World War II. This book examines the recent modifications in Harlequin romances that reflect these social changes. Alongside these revisions, however, and still central to the romances are traditional notions about women's roles. Consequently, Harlequins are ambiguous and even contradictory, a fascinating combination of the realistic problems women face in our society and escapist solutions. Romance readers are seduced with exciting but potentially distressing material – portrayals of sexual violence, for example – only to be reassured by the inevitable happy ending in which love conquers all. Harlequins, therefore, successfully balance both the tension between the conflicting psychological needs for excitement and security and the tension between traditional and "liberated" notions of women's roles. This delicate balancing act is the basis of their appeal and power.

***

To further explore the connections between society, romance and readers, it is useful to backtrack to the emergence of the novel as a literary form in eighteenth-century England. The feminine predilection for romantic fiction, its economic success and the severe criticism it has received from scholars are evident from its earliest beginnings.

Historians of the novel have linked its origins to social changes such as the growth of the reading public, the rise of the middle class and changes in the social position of women. As the middle class grew and began to turn to literature as a leisure-time pursuit, reading ceased to be the exclusively aristocratic occupation it had once been. This change had a major impact on the kind of literature being produced:

> One general effect of some interest for the rise of the novel ... seems to follow from the change in the centre of gravity of the reading public. The fact that literature in the eighteenth century was addressed to an ever-widening audience must have weakened the relative importance of those readers with enough education and leisure to take a professional or semi-professional interest in classical and modern letters; and in return it must have increased the relative importance of those who desired an easier form of literary entertainment, even if it had little prestige among the literati.[8]

The extension of the reading population to the middle class was, therefore, one factor that led to the popularity of the novel, a form that was accessible to large numbers of readers. Middle-class women in particular were drawn to novels to fill in their new-found leisure time. Up to this point, most women had been actively involved in the production of goods within the home. The growth of commerce and manufacturing industries outside the home considerably changed this situation for middle-class women, who were freed from many former domestic demands. Since they were still excluded from masculine activities outside the home like politics or business and leisure activities like sports or drinking, reading was one of the few forms of entertainment and stimulation available to them that was considered acceptably feminine. Thus the sexual division of labour within the middle-class family and society facilitated the development of the novel:

> traditional literature ... did not satisfy the hunger of the new social group; and certainly the masculine wit of eighteenth century verse and essay seemed more at home in the coffeehouse than in the boudoir where the middle classes tended to believe books were properly to be consumed. The merchant was unwilling to spend much of his time ... on the trivialities of art; such pursuits seemed to him more proper for the female members of his family.... The moment at which the novel took hold coincides with the moment of the sexual division of labor which left business to the male, the arts to the female ...[9]

This split and the large numbers of women in the reading population contributed to the focus on themes of love and marriage that often characterized these early novels. The economic changes that gave middle-class women more leisure time also made them, to a certain extent, economically superfluous. No longer necessary for the production of household goods, these women became a status symbol of wealth and idle refinement. While many working-class women might well have envied their life, middle-class women were faced with their own set of problems. Because they were largely prohibited from working in the labour force, they were under extreme economic and social pressure to marry. This pressure, coupled with the numerical surplus of women and the shortage of available men, created a preoccupation with the subject of love and marriage:

> There is ... a considerable variety of evidence to support the view that the transition to an individualist social and economic order brought with it a crisis in marriage which bore particularly hard upon the feminine part of the population. Their future depended much more completely than before on their being able to marry and on the kind of marriage they made, while at the same time it was more and more difficult for them to find a husband.[10]

Before this time, daughters were a welcome source of labour who, if they did not marry, could continue to contribute to the family's livelihood; but when it became unnecessary and unfashionable for "ladies" to work, unmarried daughters became an economic liability without status. A middle-class woman could become a governess or a companion but few women would choose the humiliation and sheer drudgery of these occupations – so vividly described in the fiction of Charlotte Bronte and Jane Austen – instead of marriage. Some unmarried middle-class women turned to writing sentimental romantic novels as one of the least disagreeable ways to earn a living. With marriage on their minds, therefore, women chose to read and write fiction that dealt with their dilemma of finding a husband and a place in society.

The popularity of novels spread quickly from England to North America. Not only were English novels such as Samuel Richardson's *Pamela* published in American editions shortly after the appearance of their British publication, but North American writers produced their own fiction as well. Again, women writers and readers and the themes of love and marriage were characteristic:

> Sentimental "domestic novels" written largely by women for women dominated the literary market from the 1840s through the 1880s. Middle-class women became in a very real sense consumers of literature.[11]

It was not very long before this time that it began to be appropriate to speak of a "literary market." Authors had previously survived through a system of patronage but this system was gradually replaced by the development of commercial booksellers who began to publish, support and influence authors and the type of literature they produced. In order to make a profit, booksellers needed to sell large quantities of books so they started to cater to the new audience's tastes, ignoring the accusation by critics that they were "turning literature itself into a mere market commodity." According to Ian Watt, the main effect of applying economic criteria to the production of literature was to encourage writers to write prose (novels) rather than verse, to write very simply to allow for a less well-educated audience and to write quickly, as they were paid for their output.[12]

The split between popular culture and "high" culture dates back, in part, to this transition from patronage to commercial enterprise. Although booksellers could afford to publish a few innovative novels that might not have broad appeal, they had to rely on "best sellers" for their basic livelihood, a state of economic affairs that remains true to this day. Many publishers are carried by their romance lines and corporate officials are only too willing to please the public by producing industry-wide 140 category romances a month.

Criticisms of women writers and popular fiction can be traced back to the early history of the novel. Elaine Showalter in her analysis of British women novelists, *A Literature of Their Own,* notes that when women first started to write for the literary market, male critics were merely patronising. By the middle of the nineteenth century, however, when it became apparent that women writers were not aberrations, male critics began to feel threatened by their increasing numbers and success and attacked them more directly. It was assumed that women writers were masculinized, dominating women and that their work was "recognizably inferior" to novels written by men. Dedicated women writers like George Eliot joined in the criticism in an attempt to dissociate themselves from the "Silly Novels by Lady Novelists" that were popular but scorned. The writing abilities of many of these widely read "lady novelists" left much to be desired but their subject matter also came under attack:

> Denied participation in public life, women were forced to cultivate their feelings and to overvalue romance. In the novels, emotion rushed

in to fill the vacuum of experience, and critics found this intensity, this obsession with personal relationships, unrealistic and even oppressive.[13]

The same criticisms are made today and concern about the effect of romances is voiced as strongly now as it was then. The attack on romances has been so sustained and intense that it warrants a closer look.

* * *

Although most academics reject popular culture, a few scholars enthusiastically study movies, comic books and roller coasters. Perhaps in reaction to the condemnation such topics usually receive, these scholars uncritically embrace their subjects. Tania Modleski, a professor of film and literature, has called attention to this tendency to aggrandize popular culture. She points out that this kind of adulation has appeared only in analyses of popular culture associated with men or with both sexes and not in analyses of popular culture associated with women – that is, romances. She thus concludes that "the double critical standard" that feminists have found in the area of literary studies is also present in the area of mass-culture studies.[14]

The double critical standard or "phallic criticism" as another writer, Mary Ellman, terms it, is a form of literary evaluation that assumes that only men can write well and that only their bold subject matter is worth writing about. In contrast, women are expected to confine their vision to small worlds – the feelings and everyday activities of their families and friends – although this restricted focus is then held against them as proof of their narrowness and inability to think about important, exterior matters. Critics who use the double critical standard are biased in their comments on women's writing, if they deign to read women authors at all.

The analysis of romance has been hampered by the double critical standard in the form of both exclusion and bias. For example, romances are essentially excluded from Cawelti's book even though it is entitled *Adventure, Mystery, and Romance.* He deals with romances in one and a half pages, the same amount of space he devotes to a discussion of alien beings![15] In 1979, the Association of American Publishers proposed the establishment of new book categories for which it would award prizes. The categories included science fiction, mysteries and westerns, but not romances, in spite of the fact that they constitute the largest single selling category in the paperback market.[16]

When romances are not ignored, they are vilified as is no other category of popular fiction, and their readers scorned as are no other readers. We do not open the pages of *The New Republic* to find articles speculating about the normalcy of mystery readers and expressing the fear that they are participating in masochistic fantasies. We do not find treatises attempting to explain why a business executive "compulsively" reads every Mack Bolan (the Executioner books published by Don Pendleton) and to ascertain whether he will be inspired by his reading to tackle the Mafia singlehandedly. Many academic devotees of science fiction, thrillers and mysteries take their own good sense and reading material for granted, in contrast to their attitudes about the "suspect" reading material of others, especially women. Harlequins appear to receive more than their share of criticism. Why?

The most plausible answer is that romances as a form of popular culture are stigmatized by the low status of their female readers and writers, as has been true since the emergence of romantic novels. In a sexist society, the association of women with a phenomenon, whether it be an occupation, a name, a political party, a play activity or literature, is enough to lessen its value and desirability. Women may cross over on a limited basis into male spheres of activity in an attempt to capture some of their prestige and power but men do not cross over into female territory. For example, in recent years, girls have thrown themselves into the formerly "masculine" pursuits of baseball and soccer but boys have not become rope-skipping enthusiasts. Moreover, if women make substantial inroads into male territory, men abandon the area rather than be tainted by the presence of women. This pattern also holds true in popular culture fiction. Although women cross over into masculine fantasies such as westerns and thrillers, men do not read romances. Their avoidance of the novels, in conjunction with women's association with them, contributes to romances' reputation as "trash." Elene Kolb comments:

> It's a question of society's apparent basic approval of both the male fantasy itself and the values inherent in the male escapist books:

power, wealth, bravery, cunning, freedom, and cool, detached sexuality; and the disregard – even contempt – with which we view the conventional feminine fantasy and the priorities of a romance novel: true love, security, fidelity, sensitivity and marriage as a woman's ultimate goal.[17]

Much criticism of romances therefore, is sexist, based as it is on acceptance of males and their fantasies as the measure of worth. This includes much feminist criticism as well, since feminists have frequently accepted the masculine orientations of adventure over romance, believing that action is more liberated than falling in love.

In order to understand the appeal of romances we must drop the critical double standard and examine romances *within their own framework*. Certainly it is possible to critique them from outside their framework. For example, besides the male fantasy and "serious" literature models already described, other perspectives point out that the books are heterosexist in their one-sided focus on male-female relationships and that they are ideological reinforcements of capitalism in their emphasis on consumerism, benign bosses and simple workers. Both of these criticisms are accurate: Harlequins *are* heterosexist; they *are* ideologically consistent with capitalism. However, my main objective is to understand the appeal of romances from the perspective of the readers. And, unlike the analysts who are opposed to the heterosexism and the capitalistic elements in both society and Harlequins, readers take the system for granted.

Recent analyses of romances have moved away from a blanket condemnation although most are still very critical of them from a feminist perspective. For example, Tania Modleski in her book on Harlequins, gothics and soap operas looks at these feminine fantasies as forms of adaptation to the "circumscribed lives" that women live in our society and opposes the automatic negative judgment that has accompanied romances in the past:

> An understanding of Harlequin Romances should lead one less to condemn the novels than the conditions which have made them necessary. Even though the novels can be said to intensify female tensions and conflicts, on balance the contradictions in women's lives are more responsible for the existence of Harlequins than Harlequins are for the contradictions.[18]

Although she also argues that the Harlequin fantasy is not always regressive, Modleski ultimately sees Harlequins as tales of feminine defeat. According to her reading, romances stress "the cost of 'revolt'" for women and portray the heroines betraying themselves, subverting their emotions. This makes the process of reading romances a destructive act in the long run and she would rather see women doing something else: "The energy women now use to belittle and defeat themselves can be rechanneled into efforts to grow and to explore ways of affirming and asserting the self."[19]

Mariam Frenier points out that Harlequin heroines have a lot of indirect power, thus debunking the myth that the new heroines are totally passive. However, she also maintains that the heroines' power is undermined and that romances sell women the traditional sex role.[20] Janet Patterson begins her analysis of Harlequins by criticizing the devaluation of women's culture, but shortly after she asks: "What is it that makes so many women dedicated to such a sadomasochistic cultural and literary experience?"[21] Her assumption that women are dedicated to sadomasochism is itself a devaluation of women's culture. Ann Snitow initially refuses to see Harlequins as anti-women's movement backlash but eventually she argues that "they feed certain regressive elements in the female experience."[22]

All of these critics provide us with valuable insights into Harlequins; nevertheless, I think they are mistaken in reading the romances as tales of defeat. To the contrary, the "new woman" featured in contemporary Harlequins gets everything she wants – economic security, a loving husband, an exciting sex life and a choice of whether or not to pursue a career. This "new woman" is able to augment traditional attitudes with emerging feminist values. Both because of the happy ending and the incorporation of some feminist issues, readers do not see Harlequins as depressing stories of female subjugation.

Another reading of Harlequins compares them to or sees them as pornography. The authors using this perspective treat the romances with varying degrees of approval and range from Ann Douglas, who is totally opposed (as is evident in her article entitled, "Soft-Porn Culture: Punishing the Liberated Woman") to Ann Snitow, who is merely unenthusiastic, as is clear when she comments that: "Read this way, Harlequins are benign if banal books ..."[23]

Although recent romances are increasingly sexual, it is not very illuminating to describe them as pornography. First of all, even the

sexual romances still place more emphasis on emotions, relationships and sensuality (touch, smells, textures, tastes and sounds) than
on the mechanics of sex. Heroines and heroes frequently have sexual
intercourse in the new romances but any action that takes place
below the waist is described with euphemisms. Compared to the
literal portrayals and the explicit "ejaculation motif" that Beatrice
Faust, in her comparative study of pornography and romances,
argues dominate pornography, Harlequins' references to "hard
thighs" and "taut masculinity" are modest.[24] A second difference
that distinguishes romances from pornography is the perspective of
the viewer or reader. Pornography frequently shows a man doing
something sexual to a woman. The viewer is instructed to perceive
the woman and the action through the male actor's eyes, to see the
woman as a sexual object. In romances, however, the reader
identifies with the woman and sees the sexual interaction through
her eyes – a significant difference. Finally, readers do not read
romances primarily for the descriptions of sex. They are interested in
sex as part of a love relationship, not "sex for sex's sake."

Nothing is added to our understanding of romances by defining
them as pornography. Certainly we should analyze the images of
sexuality in Harlequins – I do so in Chapters Five and Six – but the
negative connotations of the term pornography automatically put
limits on our understanding of those images. In addition, categoriz-
ing romances as pornography waters down the impact of the term
when it is applied to material more worthy of the epithet.

***

The attack on romances from all perspectives has been so pervasive
that Harlequin writers have felt compelled to address the issue of
stigmatized popular culture in their fiction. While they do not usually
defend romances outright, they do voice the common criticisms and
take a strong position in favour of them through their characters'
debates about the worth of popular fiction. These discussions
include not a few jibes at critics. Consider the following romance in
which the heroine, Virginia, has met a new woman friend and the
woman's cousin, a man who writes thrillers for a living:

"He's ashamed of his thrillers," she told Virginia.
"Oh, but why? It's very clever to be able to write them."

"Oh, no it isn't." Clive shook his head gloomily. "They're very popular thrillers. You should hear what the more superior critics say about them. I take it a critic could knock them off with his left hand, if he were not too busy criticising."

"Well, they make money, anyway," Jessica pointed out soothingly.

"Only aggravates the offence," declared her cousin ...[25]

This passage points out the author's awareness of the "shame" of popular culture, the belief of critics and many readers that because the books are simple fiction they are also simple to write, and the inverted elitist notion that if a book makes money, it has commercial value but no other merit. The author is understandably annoyed with these beliefs because they do not acknowledge the existence of popular culture as a separate "art form" with its own standards, creative challenges and rewards.

In response to the low status of romances, authors and publishers are attempting to upgrade the prestige and quality of their product. Professional conferences such as the much-televised Romantic Book Lovers' Conference sponsored by the newspaper, *The Romantic Times,* not only promote the genre but educate writers on proper plot construction, evocative writing styles and future trends in romances. A sense of pride and excitement pervades conferences like this, which speak of romantic authors' growing professionalism and self-assertion. Ironically these women, frequently the anathema of feminists, live out the feminist ideal of interesting work and financial independence.

With more outspokenness than in the past, the writers advocate the popular-culture cause in their fiction. In *The Loving Trap* by Daphne Clair, the heroine, who sells second-hand books in her shop, defends romances from the hero's criticisms:

"Historical dramas and love stories?" he queried ..."Do many women read that junk?"

Kyla gave him a level glance. "What do *you* read for relaxation, Mr. Nathan? The *Encyclopedia Britannica?*"

His mouth quirked a little in acknowledgement of her sarcasm. "Actually, I like a good thriller, and occasionally I read a Western. Which leaves me wide open, I suppose?"

"Yes, doesn't it?" Kyla agreed pleasantly. "If your fantasies run to mayhem and murder and the occasional smoking six-gun, do you think you can afford to criticise women for preferring to read about romantic encounters with Regency gentlemen or desert sheiks? Surely theirs is a less harmful kind of fantasy than the violent kind that men seem to indulge in?"[26]

In this passage, Clair attacks the double critical standard and points out that women primarily read romances for harmless relaxation. Her belief that popular fiction serves a valuable function for readers is echoed in the work of another long-established Harlequin author, Essie Summers. In *Through All the Years* by Summers, the heroine defends her father's mysteries and mystery readers:

> "They're written for sheer entertainment, yes, escapism if you like, but what's wrong with escapism? We all need to escape and relax these days of tension and mental stress. I've been amazed at the letters that have come from readers through Dad's publishers. From men in all walks of life saying they've enjoyed them. Even to a couple of professors and no less than three politicians! Grateful for relaxation they were ... So don't be patronising ..."[27]

One could easily substitute romances for mysteries and women for men readers in the quotation. Summers knows that romance readers also come from "all walks of life" and that housewives and physicians, secretaries and professors read them for the same purpose of relaxation.

Usually the comments on popular culture in Harlequins are just asides but in Elizabeth Graham's *Stormy Vigil,* the heroine's mistaken belief that the professor hero has prostituted himself by writing "one of those sex-filled commercially acceptable novels" is a central theme. Although Graham tries to present the case for high literary standards through her heroine, she can't resist mocking the establishment simultaneously: "But no, she couldn't really imagine that the dedicated professor of English would spend his time on trifles. It would be a literary work, meaningful and dripping with significance."[28] The touch of irreverence in the last sentence undermines the heroine's position from the beginning, and after railing against "this lightest of light fiction for the entertainment of the masses," she finally realizes that she has been elitist. She readjusts her thinking to see the worthy purpose of popular culture as giving "relaxing pleasure to millions."

Harlequin authors do not disdain good literature for, as Graham's heroine points out: "Writing a book for consumption by the masses is one thing; writing words that will last through the ages is something else again!"[29] However, they do want acceptance of romances as a legitimate form of popular culture, and I echo their sentiments. Romances may not be "dripping" with literary significance but they deserve our close attention because what they lack in this quality, they more than make up for in sociological significance, revealing as they do the fantasies of millions of women.

A consideration of the sociological significance of the images of women, men and society in Harlequins necessarily involves a comparison of fiction with reality. One cannot make informed judgments about whether a particular image is traditional or feminist, helpful or harmful, if there is no real social context for the fictional image. Nevertheless such a comparative enterprise is fraught with the possibility of simplistic, biased analysis. It seems as if romances serve as a Rorschach test to analysts; everyone sees what they want to see, depending upon their political perspective. If researchers feel that romances are by definition harmful literature for women, their perceptions of the novels are affected by this assumption. No matter what image of women is portrayed, they are inclined to criticize it in light of their belief that romances are "bad books." If they find that Harlequins portray a sex-typed work force, an unfortunately realistic portrayal, they criticize romances for perpetuating sex-role stereotypes and for not offering readers more positive role models. If, however, they discover that Harlequins portray women in a wide range of challenging, highly paid occupations, they attack them for not being realistic and for glamourizing women's labour force participation, when in reality most women are stuck in a few sex-typed jobs. Both of these charges have some truth in them but these truths are compromised by the bias of the researchers that does not allow them to see anything accurate, politically neutral or praiseworthy in the portrayals. Of course, the reverse is true as well, for Harlequin Enterprises is as unlikely to see anything harmful in its romances as a critic is to see anything redeeming.

Until now, analysts have generally applied their theoretical frameworks to romances with the intent of critiquing the novels. This method has yielded many insights but it has been unsuccessful in explaining the significance and appeal of Harlequin romances for women readers. A researcher whose goal is criticism reads a romance differently from a woman whose goal is entertainment. If we want to understand why so many women like romances, we must drop our preconceived judgments and try to read romances as readers do. We must try to understand how readers use romances and how romances fit into their everyday lives. My goal, therefore, is to explain the significance and appeal of Harlequin romances for women readers, to explore the connection between their fiction and their reality, and to analyze the fine balance between truth and fantasy that characterizes romance. My discussion is based upon the analysis of Harlequin Enterprises, which includes interviews with corporate officials; a random sample of 200 Harlequins published from 1964 through 1984; nearly 250 reader letters written to Harlequin Enterprises; and interviews with thirty romance readers.

To understand the popularity of romances in our society, I shall begin with an examination of the biggest producer of romances – Harlequin Enterprises. Until recently Harlequin dominated the romance industry and, through a combination of consumer research, business sense and editorial acumen, managed to tap women's fantasies at great financial return to themselves.

CHAPTER TWO

A CORPORATE AFFAIR

We're going gang busters.... The women love us. The dealers love us.
We love ourselves.

Richard Bellringer, vice-president,
Harlequin Enterprises, 1975

We were complacent, there's no doubt about it.

David Galloway, president,
Harlequin Enterprises, 1983

The First Romantic Book Lovers' Conference, held at the St. Regis
Hotel in New York on April 17-18, 1982, was unlike any conference
I have ever attended. Used to the rather staid atmosphere of
academic meetings, I was unprepared for the television camera
crews, the pianist playing romantic medleys in a corner of the Crystal
Ballroom and the deafening chatter of over 350 people, mostly
women, involved in the romantic fiction industry as writers, booksellers, agents, editors, publishers and readers. They were all gath-
ered to talk about romance and honour the industry's "pioneers" for
their contributions to the field. The honours ceremony opened with a
style and flourish worthy of the Academy Awards, but the conference could not generate the suspense of that Hollywood ritual
because most of the winners were foregone conclusions. For example, for publisher of category romances, who else but Harlequin?

Category romances are formula romances, regularly released, usually monthly, in a numbered series. Publishers have fairly tight control over these romances and readers frequently buy them on the

basis of brand-name loyalty to the series rather than a strongly developed preference for specific authors. Harlequin Enterprises groomed the category romance field into an economic art form.

***

Harlequin did not begin its corporate career with the intention of becoming North America's leading publisher of romantic fiction. Harlequin Enterprises was initially incorporated in Winnipeg as a privately owned company called simply Harlequin Books. In its first years of operation, it published a mixture of romance, mysteries, westerns, thrillers and non-fiction.[1] Among the famous authors published at that time were Al Cody (westerns), Agatha Christie (mysteries), Jean Plaidy, who is better known as Victoria Holt (romances), W. Somerset Maugham, and even Watergate conspirator, Howard Hunt. In contrast to the clean and respectable image that Harlequin later cultivated with its romances, many of the first selections were openly lurid and sensational, as indicated by these kinds of titles: *Lady, That's My Skull* by Carl Shannon, *The Lady Was a Tramp* by Harry Whillington and *Twelve Chinks and a Woman* by James Hadley Chase.

In 1958, Harlequin was sold to Richard and Mary Bonnycastle, who altered the course of the company. During the next ten years, they converted the company to a public corporation, changed its name to Harlequin Enterprises, moved it to Toronto, the current corporate headquarters and, most important of all, switched to publishing exclusively romances. When Mary Bonnycastle became editor, she started choosing more romances, which she considered to be "fiction 'of good taste.'"[2] Harlequin began regularly importing romances for distribution from Mills and Boon, a British publishing firm. Under this arrangement, Harlequin was allowed access to the romances already published in England by Mills and Boon. By 1964, Harlequin's romances were selling so well that it decided to switch to an exclusively Mills and Boon romantic offering and in 1971 Harlequin solidified the bond by purchasing the British company. Most Harlequins still originate in England under Mills and Boon's supervision although Harlequin has established three series in the past few years that originate in North America. Once Harlequin switched to romances, the company experienced rapid expansion, as the following table indicates:

The International Growth of Harlequin Romances

1958	Harlequin begins regularly importing romances from Mills and Boon in England
1964	Harlequin switches to an exclusively Mills and Boon romantic offering
1970	Harlequin establishes its mail order reader service for North America
1971	Harlequin buys Mills and Boon
1973	Harlequin establishes Mills and Boon Pty Limited in Australia
1975	Harlequin launches Harlequin Holland
1976	Harlequin sets up a joint venture romance publication firm in West Germany
——	Harlequin begins operations in a separate distribution centre for the USA
1977	Harlequin establishes Harlequin France, its second largest operation outside North America
1979	Harlequin sets up a joint venture romance publication firm in Greece
——	Harlequin launches Harlequin Japan, a market expected to rival the USA in size
——	Harlequin sets up a joint venture romance publication firm in Central and South America
——	Harlequin establishes operations in Sweden to market romances in Scandinavia
——	Harlequin establishes a North American sales force
1981	Harlequin launches Harlequin Italy

Source: Harlequin Enterprises Annual Report, 1980

The main area of expansion in the late 1970s was in the United States when the bulk of Harlequin's romance sales switched there from Canada. In 1969, 78 percent of sales were in Canada; by 1975, only 30 percent of total sales were there.[3] In 1977, David Sanderson, product manager for Harlequin Enterprises, told me "We tend to think of North America as being borderless" and "The border doesn't really exist for us." Illustrating his words, a large map of North America hung on the wall behind him in his corporate office.

Richard Bellringer also voiced his optimism about this borderless market: "'The American Woman, once introduced to Harlequins, is prone to succumb.... We see unlimited potential there.'"[4] Harlequin's "love conquers all" philosophy has obviously been expanded since then to include the rest of the world. It now publishes in twelve languages and its books are sold in ninety-eight countries.

Harlequin has not only increased its number of subsidiaries but has extended each of these company's operations. For example, Harlequin's North American English romance division has experienced major growth. For many years Harlequin published eight romances a month in a single series, Harlequin Romances. In 1973, Harlequin began publishing a new series, Harlequin Presents, which is generally considered to be "racier" than the regular Harlequins and which soon outstripped the original series. Harlequin Enterprises now has several series of reprints of these two lines and, encouraged by the success of Harlequin Presents, has added several other completely new series – SuperRomances, Temptations and American Romances – intended to capture different segments of the romantic fiction market. This kind of internal growth has been the rule in Harlequin's foreign operations as well. Since they began, all of the subsidiaries have increased the number of titles offered in each of the series that they publish and some have added new series.

Harlequin's past growth is evident in the corporation's vital statistics. Fiction sales jumped from 6 million books sold in 1965 to 218 million books in 1982. During the 1960s to 1970s, Harlequin reigned unchallenged with an 80 percent or more share of the North American market.[5] As a result of skyrocketing sales, net revenues jumped from nearly $8 million in 1971 to over $265 million in 1980; net earnings jumped from less than $.5 million to nearly $26 million. These prosperous years also plumped up Harlequin's current assets from about $4 million in 1970 to over $116 million in 1980 and the company experienced a 35 percent annual growth rate for over fifteen years.[6] Clearly Harlequin Enterprises' connection with romance had attained fairy tale proportions – as in the goose that laid the golden egg.

But, in the 1980s, the company's "golden egg" was transformed into Humpty Dumpty. Harlequin's high hopes and breezy confidence now lie shattered by the reality of drastically reduced profits and no one is confident that all of the corporation's men can put Harlequin Enterprises back together again. What happened? Harlequin's phenomenal success could not long escape the attention of a faltering publishing industry. As a result, almost every paperback house in North America increased its romance production or started up new romance lines. Under the onslaught of widespread competition, Harlequin's share of the market has dropped to 45 percent. Although the romance market has grown, it has not been able to absorb the glut of titles being offered and Harlequin now receives 60 percent of its books back unsold compared to a less than 25 percent return rate in its heyday.[7] In the fall of 1983, it laid off 85 workers in an attempt to save money and to stop the "plunge in profits."[8]

All signs indicate that Harlequin is a financially distressed corporation. Its present troubles should not lead us to underestimate its impact on the romantic fiction industry, however. Harlequin's original success gave birth to the industry and its rivals have not only tackled the same market, they have also adopted its personnel, book cover formats, marketing strategies and consumer research approach. At least part of the reason women read romances is that the romance industry has done everything they can not only to respond to pre-existing demand but to stimulate that demand. This chapter examines how Harlequin was able to grow from a small family-owned publishing business into a large, diversified, multinational media complex. The next chapter focuses on the growth of the romantic fiction industry, which sprung up where once a single company reigned supreme.

* * *

Long before other publishers took notice of Harlequin, it had attracted admiring attention from the Canadian government. Since it was one of the few financially viable Canadian-owned publishers, it was acclaimed in a federal government study of book publishing in Canada and held up as a model to other publishers who were advised to be as marketing conscious and as businesslike as Harlequin. Harlequin's fellow publishers, however, did not accept the comparison:

> ... for the Canadian publishers who bring out books by Mordecai Richler or Robertson Davies or Hugh Hood, Harlequin Books is an interesting curiosity, nothing more. They sell garbage, and they sell it

effectively, but the idea that one of our serious publishers might actually emulate Harlequin is – in the eyes of the publishing gents – altogether outlandish.[9]

Their protestations were not without substance. These publishers must sell various types of fiction and nonfiction with limited popular appeal as well as new and different writers with highly developed, individualized styles. The success of their publishing ventures usually depends upon the popularity of individual authors. Avid readers, too, are dependent upon the output of their favourite author, an output that usually does not exceed a book a year. In these cases, readers are probably unaware of what company is publishing their favourite author. They buy the book on the basis of the writer rather than the publisher. Consequently, publishers are hampered in their efforts to promote their products. They must push specific books or writers in an expensive, time-consuming process that has little carryover benefit for them.

In contrast, Harlequin had special advantages that allowed it to market, distribute and advertise its books with relative ease. Harlequin's success can be explained in large part by two basic factors related to these advantages: the format of the romances and an aggressive marketing program. Advisors who recommended that traditional publishers pursue a marketing program like Harlequin's did not realize that Harlequin could only advertise as it did because it sold formula fiction. Harlequin was not selling individual authors with specific appeals; Harlequin was selling its own brand name. Readers, therefore, did not have to wait for their favourite author's irregular, intermittent output. They bought books on the basis of the publisher rather than the writer.

It was in 1971 that Harlequin Enterprises first parted company with traditional publishers. After a decade, the leadership of Harlequin passed from Richard and Mary Bonnycastle to their son, Richard, who hired an unusual management team headed by W. Laurence Heisey. Heisey, eventually named *Marketing Magazine*'s Man of the Year for his innovative leadership at Harlequin during the prosperous 1970s, is a Torontonian who received his education at Harvard Business School. When he came to Harlequin, he had just spent thirteen years with Proctor and Gamble. "'I'm an old soap salesman,'" he joked,[10] but the results of his efforts to apply Proctor and Gamble's mass marketing techniques to the sale of romantic fiction was no laughing matter – unless it was a matter of laughing all the way to the bank.

The other two members of Heisey's management team, neither of whom are with Harlequin today, were Richard Bellringer and William Willson. As Bellringer points out in the following quotation, they were not bound by conventional approaches to book publishing:

> "None of the three of us came from the publishing world," recalls Bellringer, "but we recognized that we had a tiger by the tail. All we had to do was squeeze that tail and hope by heck it would jump in the right direction."[11]

One of the first things the new management did was begin an extensive research program on their product and their consumers. Since then, this has become such a regular part of corporate operations that Harlequin never launches a new product until it has first conducted consumer research studies. As a result of this research, Harlequin has a clear picture of its market and company officials are able to describe the typical Harlequin reader in terms of age, education, family income, marital status, employment and geographical location as well as her preferences for settings, characters and plots in romantic fiction.

Harlequin used its research to set up editorial guidelines designed to "give readers what they want." Obviously, Harlequin was not unique in this effort to please consumers. Ever since the development of a literary commodity market, the public has been a key arbiter of what is produced. Popular culture scholar, John Cawelti, emphasizes this point:

> ... formula stories are created and distributed almost entirely in terms of commercial exploitation. Therefore, allowing for a certain degree of inertia in the process, the production of formula is largely dependent on audience response.[12]

Nevertheless, Harlequin was certainly the first publisher to be so systematic and successful in its attempts to test consumer response and to gear its product towards its readers. Although it is less successful at present, it has not abandoned its consumer orientation. This is evident in the comments of Fred Kerner, vice-president of the Harlequin Books division, a frequent spokesman for the company until he retired in 1983. Kerner prefers to emphasize the informal, free-flowing creative process involved in the production of Harlequin Romances. Yet even he acknowledges that the overall guideline is for the author to give the reader what she wants. He also admits that: "If we ever got an overwhelming number of complaints about something, we would seriously look at it because we'd say – are we not giving the reader the total entertainment she wants?"[13] Once the new management team was in place, Harlequin Enterprises proceeded to rigorously impose business criteria on its editorial policy. As stated in the 1974 Harlequin annual report, the editors "help to direct the creativity of the authors with editorial guidelines which are market-oriented."

The result was a uniform romance product that readers could "trust." Readers did not have to discriminate between writers; they could rely on Harlequin's brand name, as the following reader reported:

> I do not have a preference in authors; each offers a different style, which is what I like. As long as a book has the Harlequin trademark, I'll read it.[14]

New writers sold almost as readily as established authors. The difference between the month's most popular title and the least popular was a mere 2 percent.[15] One of the reasons for the uniformity of sales was that many readers subscribed to a whole series of Harlequins. The company bypassed the retailer-distributor for a considerable portion of its business by selling directly to the consumer through its mail-order service. Readers could either order individual books or, as mentioned, subscribe to a series. Readers presumably benefited because they could order books without having to search through stores to find them and they got new issues before they hit the stands. Harlequin benefited because they didn't have retailer-distributor costs. In addition, subscribers through the mail-order service constituted a reliable, steady market for the company that most other publishers did not have.

This consumer brand-name loyalty also allowed Harlequins to consistently have the lowest return rates from commercial outlets in the paperback industry. *Forbes* commented on the difference between Harlequin and other publishers:

> Harlequin romances have unusually long print runs. The average paperback printing is 120,000 books; of those, the publisher can

expect to get back, unsold, 35% to 40%. Harlequin routinely prints 500,000 of a new title, of which less than 25% are returned. "Other companies print ten books to sell six," says Heisey matter-of-factly. "We print 7 1/2 to sell 6."[16]

Low book return rates meant that Harlequin could afford to sell its books at lower prices, further contributing to its edge over other publishers.

In addition, the interchangeability of Harlequin romances, despite different titles and authors, facilitated easy distribution. *The Financial Post* explained this advantage:

> Publishers must allocate to each retailer a sufficient number of volumes of each title – a tricky balancing act. Harlequin's titles, on the other hand, are almost interchangeable, thanks to editorial uniformity and a high brand identification. As Heisey cheerfully points out, it is as though Harlequin were selling one standing consumer product, rather than books.[17]

The interchangeability of the books and the conceptualization of Harlequins as a consumer product led to the realization that romances could be sold in the same places as other consumer products – the local drug store and supermarket. By setting up racks of romances in these stores, Harlequin brought its product into high traffic areas for women consumers. It increased its exposure to include women who did not usually patronize bookstores and made buying a romance as easy as buying aspirin.

In 1974, after Heisey and his management team studied Harlequin readers and streamlined their editorial guidelines to conform to reader preferences, they launched a massive television advertising campaign in the United States and Canada, costing nearly $400,000. The average increase in net sales in ten cities in the United States after the test commercials was an astonishing 79 percent.[18] Heisey promptly doubled the advertising budget for the next year and, true to his soap-selling origins, hired Compton Advertising, which also handled the Tide account, to sell Harlequins.[19]

Harlequin began with a number of ads, each aimed at a special group of women readers – the housewife and mother, the mature woman or widow, the working mother, the active young woman. The ads were based on readers' letters to the company. The following is an example of an ad directed towards a housewife and mother:

> Nap time for the twins. And now it's my turn to curl up and disappear.

With a good book. Do you know what I read? Harlequin Romances. They're well-written. Exciting ... a good love story always is. And the characters go to foreign places and see things I dream of seeing.... They're my disappearing act.

The television ads were run on network evening prime time or during afternoon soap operas. The first series of advertisements reached up to 91 percent of all television households and was viewed by 75 percent of American women at the rate of nearly six commercials a month.[20] Heisey estimated that the ads in the United States increased awareness of Harlequins by almost 25 percent.[21] The ads proved to be very effective in Canada as well. Part of the reason Harlequin had shifted attention from Canada to the United States was that it believed the Canadian market was already saturated. It discovered that this was not so:

> Three months later it is obvious that the TV ads are having an enormous impact. Eaton's in Winnipeg reports that it has shifted its housewares department to make room for an area devoted to the Harlequins. Simpsons store in Toronto turned over its entire display inventory three times in its first eight days of operation (about 2,500 books).[22]

The company has steadily increased its advertising budget each year until it now spends nearly $2 million a year on television campaigns.

The advertising campaign was also carried to popular magazines, particularly the women's magazines. For example, a full-page ad in the *Ladies Home Journal* read: "Remember when you first fell in love? Relive that special excitement ... every time you read a Harlequin Romance. Come into the world of Harlequin novels ... and be a part of a wonderful dream."[23] Advertising was coupled with a giveaway program. In 1973, dealers were sent two million free copies of a romance which they were to sell for 15 cents (the regular price at that time was 60 cents) in an attempt to get new readers.[24] Other promotional ventures done on a contractual basis include a complete romance published in *Good Housekeeping* that was followed by a coupon the reader could send in to receive a free Harlequin; a romance packed in the large-size box of Kotex feminine napkins and Bio-Ad detergent; romances given away to customers at McDonald's restaurants on Mother's Day; romances given away with purchases of Avon products and Jergens lotion and a free romance given in exchange for a coupon found on the bottom of Ajax cans.[25] This whole give-away campaign was based on the assumption that Harlequins are "addictive." This has been frequently stated by representatives of the company:

"We know that once we get a reader hooked she comes back for more."[26]

"We know through research and experience that Harlequins are a very addictive line to readers of all ages."[27]

"The company ... provides addictive reading for women of all ages."[28]

This line of thinking has also been evident in Harlequin's advertising directed at the retailer. Harlequin ads appearing in trade magazines such as the *Progressive Grocer, Supermarket News* and *Book Trade* emphasized the repeat potential of the loyal Harlequin reader:

Our regular reader, bless her. Why does she – and millions of other women like her – come back to Harlequin displays all over the country, week after week? .... You're missing a sure thing if you're not offering her the books she loves – and buys – week after week.[29]

Even the romances themselves served as a vehicle for further advertisement. Harlequins often contained order blanks and coupons for other Harlequin series or books. For example, when Harlequin made a movie, *Leopard in the Snow,* from one of its romances, it inserted advertisements in 15 to 20 million books published over a four-month period before the movie's release.[30]

The latest advertising gimmick from Harlequin combines a clever understanding of the needs of both television news programs and avid readers – reader thank-you parties, another industry first. The parties have been set up in over twenty cities in North America and not incidentally receive ample media attention. The luncheon parties all follow an identical agenda although they are each played out by the personnel – Fred Kerner, Katherine Orr, consumer relations director and a Harlequin author – as if the action was spontaneous. Readers are chosen by a lottery drawn from responses to a local newspaper ad. Approximately two hundred women then converge upon a local hotel dining room for a free lunch, speeches and free books given away in pink shopping bags. The local media are informed of the party well in advance and Harlequin has concocted a number of eminently filmable events – like Fred Kerner pretending to be a bride and throwing a wedding bouquet into a crowd of readers, or readers with wedding anniversaries that month cutting a huge cake shaped like a Harlequin Romance. Everyone goes away from the party happy – readers because they feel appreciated, authors because they feel recognized, television news teams because they have a snappy, up-beat human interest story, and certainly Harlequin because it has solidified consumer loyalty and received a lot of relatively cheap publicity.

Harlequin has also sponsored two contests, one in conjunction with Delta Air Lines, that have been nationally advertised. The sweepstakes prizes include vacations to "exotic locales," a tie-in with the typically "exotic" settings of Harlequin Romances. Again, these contests both heighten reader involvement and create spin-off publicity.

The standardized format of its books and the extensive marketing program that became an integral part of the company's operations under Bonnycastle's new management team separated Harlequin Enterprises from traditional publishers. In fact, instead of being classified as simply a book publishing firm, Harlequin is more appropriately defined as a marketing company. It identifies itself as such and that is the orientation that has guided both its romance operations and its expansion outside the romance market.

The fifteen years of prosperity that Harlequin experienced in the late 1960s and throughout the 1970s led to its corporate growth. Corporations typically experience four periods of growth:

> At first, expansion is characterized by diversification. The profits which are generated through the day-to-day operations of the company are invested in other business concerns...
>
> Market control and control of the various stages of production become the principal criteria for further growth. Market control is achieved through the acquisition of competing firms – a process known as horizontal integration.
>
> While horizontal integration refers to control over a particular segment of the industry, it does not necessitate any changes in the production process. However, since profit is generated at each step in the production cycle, a corporation that controls many or all steps in the process can compound its profit. This pattern of investment, known as vertical integration, occurs when a corporation attempts to extend its control over all production stages.
>
> The final stage ... is consolidation. This occurs when a corporation develops internal strategies to maximize its profits through the reduction of costs, the elimination of redundancies, and the centralization of management.[31]

These periods occur roughly in order but they overlap and a company may be diversifying at the same time that it is extending its control over a specific market. Harlequin's growth fits this model. It has experienced diversification, horizontal integration, vertical integration and is now in the process of consolidation. Throughout this process, the emphasis on marketing has been the glue that has bound the organization together.

One of Harlequin's first attempts at diversification was the 1970 formation of an educational supplies company, Scholar's Choice, which operated primarily in the United States and Canada. This company produced Canadian Studies programs, children's stories, metric learning kits, puzzles and other learning aids. By the end of the decade, however, this branch of Harlequin had fallen on hard times and the 1979 Harlequin annual report indicated that : "The industry would not attract Harlequin investment today, for the institutional market has been significantly weakened by declining school enrollment and budgetary restrictions."[32] Harlequin tried to keep the company afloat by extending its potential market from the schools to include direct sales to parents in retail outlets but this proved unsuccessful and Scholar's Choice eventually folded.

Another pursuit that diversified Harlequin's scope of business activities while still utilizing its mass marketing skills was popular magazines. In 1976, Harlequin bought Ideals Publishing Corporation, an American book and magazine publisher. Ideals published what it called "inspirational magazines," slick glossy magazines featuring colourful pictures accompanied by poetry and sentiment. It also produced greeting cards and relatively cheap, short, thematic cookbooks – for example, an all-American cookbook and a Christmas kitchen cookbook. Ideals also marketed a series of children's stories and, through an acquisition of its own, do-it-yourself books.

Continuing to expand its magazine production, Harlequin purchased the Laufer Company in California in 1978. This subsidiary put out the adult gossip magazine, *Rona Barrett's Hollywood* and teen idol magazine, *Tiger Beat* and its sister publication, *Tiger Beat Star*. The production of these magazines was linked to Harlequin's production of romances through their female audiences and their emphasis on male fantasy objects, although teen idol heroes are quite unlike typical Harlequin heroes. Teen idols are young, fun to be with, ingenuous, and very sweet. The "S-E-X-Y color pinups" in *Tiger Beat* reveal soft-looking, beardless, non-threatening young boys. As soon as teen idols reach manhood and develop noticeable chest hair, they are dumped, unless they cultivate a boyish, teddy-bear personality. In contrast, Harlequin heroes are big, strong, tough, intimidating men. However, the difference between teen idols and Harlequin heroes may be more apparent than real since both magazines and books present unobtainable male figures to be loved by female readers. Moreover, Harlequin Enterprises has been willing to make money off either the androgynous or the macho male. Obviously they are not ideologically bound to one male sex-role model; they sell what readers will buy.

After several magazine acquisitions, Harlequin formed a new division based in New York with the goals of building

> a significant and profitable presence in the North American consumer-magazine industry. Important parallels between this industry and Harlequin's paperback operations suggest that consumer magazines can play a productive role in our overall diversification program.[33]

The company then purchased *ARTnews, Antiques World* and *Photo Life*. In addition, it published *Snow Goer* in Canada under a licensing arrangement with the Webb company, an American firm, and provided management services to *Weight Watcher's Magazine* in a joint venture with American Baby Inc.

Harlequin ventured farther afield in its 1980 purchase of the Miles Kimball Company of Oshkosh, Wisconsin, a direct mail-order marketing firm that sells a collection of curios such as engraved chewing gum cases, rotary nose hair clippers and flamingo lawn ornaments. Miles Kimball's emphasis on mail-order marketing blended into Harlequin's mail-order romance business and there is a parallel in the products they produce and the reasons for their success. Through skillful marketing, both companies rely on the glamourization of everyday life and relentless optimism to sell their products. Any company that can sell personalized car floor mats with the claim that they "lend distinction and class to your auto, truck, or RV" is a company after Harlequin's own heart.[34]

At the same time that Harlequin was diversifying, it was also attempting to extend its dominance in the book publishing industry by establishing new publishing companies and book lines as well as taking over competing firms. Harlequin has continually tried to duplicate its success with romances in other areas of fiction, using the same techinques of marketing, management and sales. For about a year and a half in the mid-1970s, Harlequin published a monthly science fiction series under the name of Laser Books but it never achieved a respectable profit margin and was phased out. In 1980, Harlequin tentatively launched Raven House, a mystery series. According to the annual report of the year:

... Our market research has indicated that further refinements are needed before a wide-scale retail launch is undertaken. Modifications accordingly were introduced.... We are pursuing our investment program with regard to the development of other new series; once these newly developed series achieve the high standards of editorial excellence prescribed, they will be launched and marketed where suitable through the extensive international network we have at our disposal.[35]

Harlequin already had a subsidiary involved in publishing mystery fiction in Germany and hoped to build an international distribution network as it had for the romances. It invested in an advertising campaign that bet that mystery readers could be seduced as profitably as romance readers, but the books were panned by reviewers and readers left them on the shelves. The series was canceled because there wasn't a high enough turnover. A Harlequin representative explained to me that the company was unwilling to wait for its mystery writers to gain a following, a decision consistent with its focus on brand-name fiction rather than individual authors.

In addition, no longer content with only women readers' loyalties (besides constituting nearly 100 percent of the romance market, women also buy 65 percent of the mysteries sold[36]), Harlequin decided to woo male readers. According to a *Business Week* interview with Harlequin's vice-president of the North American division, William Gaspero, Harlequin believed that men constitute a large, untapped market for escape reading that features heroes like James Bond or Nick Carter. Gaspero indicated that their market research looked promising so the company began publishing three adventure series under the Gold Eagle label. All three of these series are written or co-authored by Don Pendleton, the popular writer of over forty books in the Executioner series, which Harlequin stole from Pinnacle books amid much litigation. The Executioner series has been translated into twelve languages and sold in 125 countries.

The hero of Pendleton's books is Mack Bolan, an ex-soldier dedicated to fighting crime and corruption, striving for ultimate justice either within or beyond the law. The books are narrated from Bolan's perspective in a terse staccato style. Here is a quote from *Return to Vietnam,* number 43 in the series:

It would soon be dawn.
A New day.
In a new war.
But Mack Bolan, the Executioner in combat black, was prepared for whatever that day might bring.
Victory.
Death.
Or both.[37]

Another example, even more abbreviated, also included Pendleton's favourite expletive:

Yeah.
Nam.
The jungle.[38]

Pendleton's stark narration is in contrast to the detailed loving attention paid to weapons and death:

The guards released one good shout and one good whistle. Then Bolan was squeezing off rounds, muting these two forever.
The guard to his left had his mouth wide open to repeat the barked command. He fielded a 9mm projectile through the mouth instead. There was no entry wound: but as the man went into his tumbling death dance, his head became wreathed in a gory mist from what must have been one massive exit wound.
Guard number two let the whistle drop from his mouth. He was still pulling up his AK-47 on Bolan when the Beretta's second message of death punched his right eyeball out through the back of his head. [39]

I kept a body count as I read *Return to Vietnam.* In the space of four hours, the time period of the story, over fifty people were killed, yet Bolan is referred to, in all seriousness, as "the gentle giant."

The Executioner series dwells on violence as extensively as Harlequin Romances dwell on love. Murders and assassinations are described as frequently as kisses and embraces in the love stories. Both types of fiction use some of the same romanticizing language – descriptive adjectives, vivid metaphors, and euphemisms that insulate the reader from the realm of reality.

The other two Gold Eagle series, Able Team and Phoenix Force, are spin-offs starring groups of men trained and commanded by the Executioner. Harlequin Enterprises maintains that the popular television show, *The A-Team,* is a direct rip-off of its series and that its popularity has led to increased sales for the Gold Eagle books, so much so that the company has added another two series, Dagger and SOBs (Soldiers of Barrabas).

All five of these series are produced regularly in numbered releases, like the romances. The Executioner series is based on the appeal of one author, a bit of a departure from Harlequin's usual reliance on tightly edited brand-name fiction. Pendleton was well-known before Harlequin began to publish him so there was no need to develop a following for the series. Harlequin borrowed heavily upon Pendleton's reputation to launch its other Gold Eagle books and, according to the company, these lines are very successful. Harlequin has apparently been able to duplicate its success in selling female fantasy fiction in its efforts to sell male fantasy fiction.

All of the acquisitions described were part of Harlequin's plan to diversify and to pursue horizontal integration by incorporating companies that could draw upon the publishing and marketing skills it had developed. It also expanded in a process of vertical integration, which occurs when a corporation attempts to control each step of the production process, a move that lessens dependence on other corporations and compounds internal profits.

Harlequin became more vertically integrated primarily by taking over more and more of its sales and distribution systems. The first step towards vertical integration was taken when Harlequin bought Mills and Boon, its source of romances. The next step was the establishment of its extensive mail-order business, which completely bypassed the retailer-distributor. For most of its sales, however, Harlequin was dependent upon its distributors – Har-Nal Distributors in Canada, a company owned 50 percent by Harlequin and 50 percent by New American Library and, more importantly, Simon and Schuster's Pocket Books Division in the United States. In the late 1970s, Harlequin dissolved both of these arrangements and took over its own distribution. A sales organization was formed, employing 130 people, to promote the sales of Harlequin products in North America. The ramifications were tremendous, partly because this action gave the company the opportunity to develop its marketing and distribution skills, and partly because Simon and Schuster was unwilling to let the romance profits go. It developed its own romance series, Silhouette Romances, which became Harlequin's main rival.

In addition to distribution and sales, Harlequin increasingly eliminated other publishers who previously had translation rights to Harlequin Romances. Harlequin began to publish in foreign languages through its own subsidiaries.

Another area of vertical integration that Harlequin has explored is movie production. In 1977, Harlequin produced its first movie, *Leopard in the Snow,* from a romance by Anne Mather. The film, costing over $1 million and starring Keir Dullea and Susan Penhalgion, was released in 1978 and was promptly panned by the critics. Harlequin, however, used to unfavourable critical response to its romances, was interested only in audience reaction. Heisey expressed his hopes for the film by stating that: "We would like to be to women in the romantic field as Disney is to children."[40] *Leopard in the Snow* was not financially successful enough to warrant a successor but the company has not totally abandoned the idea of producing movies. Instead it simply switched its focus from the movie studio to the television studio and gave an option for twelve TV films based on Harlequin romances to a Los Angeles production company, Newland-Raynor.[41]

It is difficult to translate a Harlequin-type romance from the written medium to the screen. In the attempts I have seen, the filmmakers relied heavily on intrusive mood music and a narrator used to tie the story together, to create atmosphere and to speak the characters' thoughts. The characters were stiff and unreal, and altogether the film lacked the flow and the vividness of the written romances. One reason for this is that readers can suspend disbelief more easily than viewers and much of the dialogue that is evocative in written form sounds ridiculous if actually spoken, and if omitted, robs the story of much of its feeling. For example, a reader imaginatively involved in a romance accepts the hero huskily breathing the following line: "I can see by your passion-darkened eyes that you want me." But the line can only sound stilted on film. This problem will be exaggerated the more sexual the romances become – and that is certainly the trend – because not only do the writers use a lot of euphemism and metaphor, they also describe intense internal emotion and bodily sensation, which are difficult to capture on screen. However, some romance writers are now writing scenes as if they might be played in a movie, anticipating the transformation of book into film. If writers and movie directors can successfully create this transformation, we may expect to see regularly released (and numbered?) Harlequin made-for-television movies in the future.

From this brief history, one can see that Harlequin Enterprises grew through diversification, horizontal integration and vertical integration into a large, multinational corporation. As it prospered, it attracted the attention of other expanding corporations looking for profitable acquisitions and in 1976, a controlling interest in Harlequin was bought by Torstar Ltd., a Toronto-based newspaper and magazine publisher. Together they form a media complex that is included in any study of dominant Canadian companies because of its size and scope. It ranks 131 of the top 500 industrials ranked by sales, 119 ranked by assets and 180 ranked by net income.[42] The corporation produces newspapers including the *Toronto Star,* the largest daily newspaper in Canada; romantic fiction accounting for 28 percent of all Canadian paperbacks sold[43] and 10 to 12 percent in the United States[44]; magazines; educational materials; films; and computerized information data links. Although Canadian based, it is an international organization with both subsidiaries and joint ownership ventures in numerous countries.

The Torstar company is an expanding complex, but it is small compared to some of its indigenous and international competition. On its home ground, for example, it is led by both Southam Inc. and Thomson Newspapers. All three of these companies, however, are simply media companies and are dwarfed by a truly diversified international competitor like Gulf and Western, the sixty-first largest industrial in the United States. This company owns Simon and Schuster, the publisher that produces Silhouette Romances. Gulf and Western has sales and assets of nearly $6 billion a year, compared to Torstar's $.5 billion. Producing everything from municipal traffic control systems to the Miss Universe and Miss U.S.A. pageants, Gulf and Western's brand names include Catalina swimwear, Simmons mattresses, Oscar de la Renta, Famous Players Theatres, Fruit of the Loom, Paramount Pictures and Dutch Master cigars.[45] Obviously Torstar has a long way to go before it reaches the mammoth proportions of Gulf and Western but it has achieved considerable growth and diversification through its purchase of Harlequin Enterprises and its subsidiaries.

Initially, Torstar made no changes in Harlequin's operations. A corporate executive in 1977 told me that one never saw Torstar people around Harlequin's office and that Harlequin's operations were completely independent. However, as Torstar bought more Harlequin stock, more Torstar representatives were appointed to Harlequin's board of directors. Harlequin's acquisitions were noticeably compatible with Torstar's interests in magazines and film. In 1981, Harlequin published its last independent annual report and dissolved its own board of directors. The company is now undergoing consolidation into Torstar's operations. The parent has taken over the management of all the subsidiaries that Harlequin acquired in its growth process and, ironically, Harlequin is now back to where it began: publishing popular books. (Romances still account for 80 percent of the company's book business.[46])

* * *

Since Harlequin is a company that made its fortune from romances which are read by women, it is instructive to look at the role women have played in the company. The first fact that strikes one's attention is that there never was a woman on Harlequin's board of directors. This is not surprising, considering that women have traditionally been excluded from the powerful institutions and positions in our society. Dorothy Smith, a Canadian sociologist and feminist, has pointed out that:

> In the various social apparatuses concerned with the production and distribution of ideas and images ... it is men who occupy the positions of authority, men who predominate, and men who control what enters the discourse by occupying the positions which do the work of gatekeeping and the positions from which people and their "mental products" are evaluated.[47]

Smith qualifies this by pointing out that women have not been excluded from certain areas of the production of ideas that deal with domestic concerns:

> Women have of course had access to and used the limited and largely domestic zone of women's magazines, television programs, women's novels, poetry, soap operas, etc. But this *is* a limited zone. It follows the contours of their restricted role in the society.[48]

Harlequin Enterprises should fit into this limited zone of permissible female participation but, as indicated, women have been noticeable primarily for their absence in the important positions within the corporation. Ironically, Harlequin's male dominance has been particularly evident in its Book Publishing Division, which produced Harlequin Romances with a management staff of twenty-one men and no women.

There is one woman in Harlequin's corporate office at management level, the director of personnel. Miles Kimball, when acquired, had a woman chair and a woman vice-president of finance. Torstar has two women on a fourteen-person board.[49] Those five women are the only women in upper management in the Harlequin-Torstar complex. Furthermore, three of these five are in positions of power because of direct family ownership connections. For example, the chair of Miles Kimball is Alberta Kimball. If women make it there at all, they generally get on boards of directors through inherited power.

Nevertheless, it would be inaccurate to say that women have been totally without influence within the company. Besides the women just mentioned, Mary Bonnycastle, in the company's early years, markedly affected the development of Harlequin when she chose to publish the romances that led to its growth. Harlequin's editorial positions have continued to be staffed largely by women, both in England at Mills and Boon and in the last few years, in the new North American romance operations. These women make key editorial decisions about what to publish and whom to publish. They are, therefore, in gatekeeper positions. A further consideration is the fact that all of Harlequin's approximately two hundred writers (with a few exceptions) are women. At the baseline, it is women who produce Harlequin's romance product.

Attention to the numbers of women present is not sufficient to adequately understand the extent of their inclusion or exclusion from these kinds of organizations, however. For women are inevitably concentrated in the least powerful positions even when they are included: "the closer the positions come to policy-making or innovation in ideological forms, the smaller proportion of women," says Smith.[50] This has been and is still true of women's positions at Harlequin. For example, although Mary Bonnycastle acted as editor, it was her husband Richard who headed the company and her son Richard who took over after his father's death. Neither of her daughters have played dominant roles in the company. In addition, although the women editors are powerful from a writer's perspective, it is Alan Boon who is Group Editorial Director of Fiction. He sits on Torstar's board of directors; they do not. At Harlequin's corporate office, the director of personnel may be a woman but this position means that the majority of people under her authority are clerical and secretarial staff members who are women even more removed from policy-making positions.

The relative positions of men and women within the corporate structure are perfectly illustrated by two pictures that appear in the company's annual reports. The first picture in the 1979 report features nine managerial men, uniformly dressed in dark suits and white shirts, standing on an open staircase in a white-walled, white-carpeted room. The other picture, in the 1980 annual report, features eighteen women working on a mail-order shipping line at Miles Kimball. In contrast to the elegant simplicity of the first picture, this one reveals a clutter of hanging fluorescent lights, piles of boxes and an assembly-line shelf at the level of the women's heads. The women, dressed in jeans and blouses, have their backs to the camera. Their hands and heads are a blur as they pack the boxes in front of them. These two pictures demonstrate the reality of women's positions at Harlequin Enterprises: while women are present, they are in the least powerful positions.

Smith makes a related point that men's work is deemed important but women's work is not. Men constitute an inner circle to which women are seldom admitted. She gives an example:

> It seems that women as a social category lack proper title to membership in the circle of those who count for one another in the making of ideological forms. To identify a woman novelist as a woman novelist is to place her in a special class outside that of novelists in general.[51]

If this is true of women novelists, it is even more true of women novelists who are writing romances, or "women's literature." As a result, Harlequin Romances, the direct product of women's work as novelists, are commonly regarded to be "garbage." The significance of Harlequin Enterprises, however, has been an entirely different matter. The corporate board, entirely composed of men and their work – the management and control of the corporation – has had complete credibility. The novels may be considered to be trash and the women who read and write them simple-minded, but there has been no questioning of the skill and ability of the men and the corporation.

Although these attitudes are prevalent and perpetuated, Harlequin Enterprises and its romances should not be seen as a "male conspiracy" carried out to reinforce male dominance and female subordination. First, the company does not exist in a vacuum, but in a sexist society that has been reflected in Harlequin's corporate structure. Harlequin Enterprises faced certain organizational imperatives. Boards of directors are best composed of wealthy, powerful, well-connected people who can facilitate the company's goal of profitable growth. In our society, these people are most likely to be male. Not surprisingly then, males are most likely to appear on boards of directors. Harlequin is by no means alone in having had an exclusively male board. It should be clearly understood, however, that the perpetuation of sexism is one effect of the acceptance of this state of affairs and Harlequin Enterprises took no steps to change the sex composition of its board.

A second objection to the male conspiracy theory is that Harlequin's overt goal, as stated in official policy, is to sell romance (and products other than romance) to make a profit, not to sell romance for sexism's sake. This objection does not deny that if sexism sells, then Harlequin will be only too pleased to market it. It is also true that as men and as corporate heads employing relatively cheap female labour, they experience benefits from sexism that are certainly not to be discounted, but profit based on sales is their primary goal. If images of strong women who are unwilling to abandon their careers for love and traditional marriages sell, Harlequin will be equally happy to market that.

Harlequin Enterprises cannot be seen, therefore, as an exclusively male conspiracy designed to consciously perpetuate sex-role inequality. This is too simplistic; however, Harlequin has reproduced the sexism of our society in its corporate organization. Its sexism is rooted in the institutional sexism in our society wherein discrimination is perpetuated not so much by individual men with evil intentions as by social structural elements like the inheritance of private property, the need for cheap labour and the drive for profits. Harlequin must make money and expand or it will be driven out of business by other corporations who will, as it is beginning to discover. The slogan of the corporate world could very well be the line from the rock and roll song that goes: "If I don't do it, somebody else will."

***

Harlequin's past history has been a corporate romance complete with Mr. Right and the golden glow, but will the Harlequin story have a happy ending? *Forbes* predicted otherwise in a March 1982 article entitled, "Heartbreak Comes to Harlequin." Other industry observers are also cautious about the company's future. Why the change? Why has Harlequin lost its aura of romance?

Some analysts trace the decline back to the Torstar takeover, which was completed in 1981. Lea Hansen, communications analyst with Dominion Securities Ltd. in Toronto, felt the merger would work: "'The two management teams are much less reluctant about getting along than they were two years ago.'"[52] But not everyone was enthusiastic about the new collaboration. Some experts voiced concern that the total takeover by Torstar would "blunt [Harlequin's] management drive."[53] Torstar's management has been criticized for its unimaginative handling of the *Toronto Star,* which has been losing ground to both the *Toronto Sun* and the *Globe and Mail.* Analyst Avner Mandelman commented that: "'The Star's management has been trying to arrest the decline of that paper for quite a while. Yet it had been reacting to change, and initiating very little.'"[54] Analysts hoped that Torstar's disappointing performance would not be imitated by Harlequin but industry observers were soon starting to make similar criticisms of that company. For example: "Harlequin is a classic case of missing out on a changing market."[55]

Torstar had expected Harlequin to contribute between 70 and 80 percent of its total profit,[56] but Harlequin has not lived up to these expectations by any means. Critics of the Torstar takeover may have felt some vindication when they read Torstar's nine-month report following the purchase:

> For the nine months ended Sept. 30, 1981, net income, operations declined 88% from the corresponding year-earlier period. The decline was attributed primarily to a decrease in earnings of Harlequin as well

as higher interest rates related to the company's increased investment in Harlequin and others.[57]

Harlequin's earnings were down because it had more book returns than ever before. The reason is that it is no longer a unique publisher of category romance fiction and it has lagged behind other publishers in responding to evolving consumer tastes. Like Torstar, which has reacted to market pressures but initiated little, Harlequin has followed a conservative editorial policy that met women's demand for romance in the past but did not anticipate the rapid developments in the market that have taken place in the last few years. The next chapter will examine these industry changes and take a look at Harlequin's competition for women readers of romance.

*

CHAPTER THREE

RIVALS AND WRITERS

"You have to chase after the market," a Warner Books representative said. "The good ladies are the market today."

N.R. Kleinfield
New York Times

Could these talented women who failed to produce literature of the first rank have done better? If so, why didn't they?

Nina Baym
Woman's Fiction

Harlequin Enterprises was the inspiration for a host of industry imitators and rivals. Other publishers could not help but notice Harlequin's peak 1977 aftertax profits, which were almost five times the mass market paperback world average.[1] Comparisons are an inevitable part of the business world and when they reveal that one branch of a business is vastly more profitable than another, the market is promptly flooded with look-alike products produced by companies hoping to cash in on the profits. The success of Harlequin could not have come at a better time for that publisher because while it was making it to the top, other publishers were going under in a slow book market. A 1981 *Business Week* report succinctly summarized the difference: "Last year the number of mass market paperbacks sold in the U.S. *declined* slightly to 500 million, but romance sales *rose* about 10%."[2] Consequently, publishers rediscovered romance and women readers: "Publishing people figure that women account for as much as 70% of sales. Not surprisingly, then, publishing houses are catering to women as never before."[3] Dell vice-president Ross Claiborne, in a moment of exuberance, declared that printing romances is "'a license to print money.'"[4] Romance readers, an estimated twenty million strong, are responsible for half a billion dollars of paperback publisher's annual sales.[5] No other single category of fiction approaches the size of this market.

These statistics encouraged many publishing firms to increase their romance production. According to a 1981 *Publishers Weekly* special report on romance fiction:

> Outside of Harlequin, where 100% of the title output is romance fiction [this is no longer true], the rest of the paperback houses claim an 8%-40% range of annual title output is romance fiction. Most of the publishers with less than 15% title output in romances are looking for ways to expand their romance fiction business.[6]

And expand they did. In 1980, Harlequin had only one major rival — Silhouette Romances — and between the two of them, they published fifteen titles a month. Three years later, eight major publishers fought to sell 140 category romance titles a month.[7]

This growth has not been accomplished without a lot of bitter battles. Corporate court suits have been followed by countersuits, and Harlequin has been either the plaintiff or the defendant in many of the cases. The action that started the war was Harlequin's decision to market its own books rather than continue to use Simon and Schuster's Pocket Books division. Pocket Books immediately sued Harlequin in the United States courts for loss of $50-million-a-year revenues and started its own line of romance under the Silhouette imprint, which looked remarkably like Harlequin's.[8] Harlequin, in turn, charged Simon and Schuster with unfair competition and asked that Silhouette be restrained from using the covers that so closely resembled Harlequins, a plea that was granted. Simon and Schuster retaliated with still another suit charging Harlequin with attempting to block the marketing and distribution of Silhouettes.

The keen competition between the two companies is also evident in the tug-of-war over corporate executives and writers. Silhouette hired P.J. Fennell, Harlequin's vice-president of sales and marketing, to be its president. He did not stay at Silhouette long but it was long enough to steal four of Harlequin's leading authors, including Janet Dailey, the second best-selling woman writer in the world, and to introduce to Silhouette most of Harlequin's proven sales techniques — like television advertising and international distribution.

While Silhouette was stealing an executive and authors from Harlequin, Harlequin was busy stealing personnel from Pinnacle Books after an abortive attempt to buy the company. Harlequin was stopped in this acquisition by the u.s. justice department, which indicated that it would lodge an antitrust suit against Harlequin if it succeeded in its takeover attempt. (One of the reasons Harlequin turned to the American market was that it was fed up with Canadian governmental regulations of business and felt that the American government was more understanding. One wonders if it is still so enthusiastic.) Since it could not buy the company, Harlequin hired Andrew Ettinger, its editor-in-chief, and Don Pendleton, Pinnacle's author of the Executioner series, followed him. Pinnacle sued both Ettinger and Harlequin for wrongful enticement but the courts eventually dismissed the suit. On the romance front, Harlequin hired editor Vivian Stephens away from Dell to edit its new American series and one of Dell's popular Candlelight authors, Alice Morgan, followed.

In short, Harlequin has been in court since 1979 defending itself against charges and pressing charges of its own against other corporations, attempting to expand its influence in new, potentially prosperous fiction markets while preserving its domination over the romance market. The latter has not been easy to do because Harlequin's imitators have also become innovators. The company has to compete not only against more publishers producing nearly identical romances but against publishers producing "new" and "improved" romances that seem fresh and appealing to readers.

***

The romance series have in common that they are all formula fiction. As one commentator put it: "A category romance is a terra cognita – a safe, known quantity devoid of shocking surprises – and must be instantly recognizable as such."[9] Category romances are easily identified by their standardized covers; each publisher has its own logo, colour and layout. Harlequin's Presents series features a white cover with an oval picture of the hero and heroine in the bottom half of the cover; Silhouette's Desire series has red and black covers with an oval picture of the hero and heroine locked in an embrace that takes up most of the cover space. Frequently the book is also numbered, an indication that it is but one in a regularly released series. The length of most of the books runs between 190 and 250 pages. In other words, they are short, predictable reads. In all of these characteristics, the new romances imitate Harlequins, the forerunner in the field.

In the last few years, however, publishers have struggled to find the angle or gimmick that will make their romance product stand out of the crowd. Consequently, Beatrice Small, author of *Skye O'Malley,* notes that: "... subtly the genre began to break up into subcategories, and the romance books began to have more heads than a hydra."[10] The romance industry has developed four types of variation, four specialized appeals, that vary in terms of time period of the story, age of heroine, degree of sexuality and degree of realism.

The first dimension of variation is the time period of the story. Most categories are contemporary romances although a few companies publish historical romances in series. These novels, usually set in the English Regency period, are chiefly non-sexual comedy-of-manners stories with a fair amount of attention paid to period language, costumes and customs. Harlequin developed a line of historical romances to capture some of this market but its historical series never attained great success. The *Romantic Times* reports that Harlequin has put its historical series "on hold" for the time being.[11] Many other publishers have also discontinued their historical category romances.

The second dimension of variation within category romantic fiction is the age of the heroine. Traditionally, heroines have been young women in their late teens or early twenties. The majority of the current Harlequin romance heroines still fall within the twenty to thirty-year-old range, but other publishers and other romance lines within Harlequin Enterprises have strayed from this formula. Signet/NAL's September Romances feature no heroine under forty. Harlequin's American series follows suit: "Heroine – Should be mature American Woman no younger than 26 years old. She *can* be older." Editorial guidelines for series like Signet's Adventures in Love romances that do not specify age indicate that the heroine should at least "have a sense of maturity that manifests itself in her dedication and goals."

Bifurcation has occurred in the opposite direction as well: heroines have also gotten younger. At least six publishers are now producing teenage romances geared to the twelve to sixteen-year-old reading market. Stories about lost, homeless ponies and faithful dogs were replaced in the 1960s by "the problem novel," which focused on topics like divorce, alcoholism and premarital sex. These have been pushed aside in the 1980s by teenage love stories. Sales, according to *Publishers Weekly,* have been "staggering."[12] The rush into this field was led by that well-known publisher of children's books, Scholastic Inc., which produced several series of teenage romances – Wildfire, Wishing Star and Windswept – which, in turn, have been imitated by publishers such as Dell with Young Love, Bantam with Sweet Dreams and Silhouette with First Love Romances. All of these romances follow the same basic parameters:

> The manuscript generally has 40,000-50,000 words. The heroine is 15-17, the boy slightly older. The story is told from the girl's point of view. The action takes place in a suburb or small town. There is no explicit sex or profanity. Although romance is the focus, the story may also deal with other adolescent problems. The ending is upbeat.[13]

The third area of variation is the degree of sexuality incorporated into the story and the sexual responsiveness of the heroine. Romances have traditionally favoured pure virginal heroines and some books still retain them. Innocent heroines are one reason for the popularity of the romances of Barbara Cartland, the best-selling woman writer in the world. Her books are melodramatic morality plays in which the virginal heroine defends her honour from the lecherous rake long enough to be rescued by the sexually-experienced-but-pure-in-spirit hero. Cartland's style is as breathless as Pendleton's is terse. For example, in *Vote for Love,* an anti-suffragette romance, the heroine, Viola, an "exquisite, fragrant and perfect" "little white violet," declares her love for the hero:

> "But you are so ... magnificent, so ... wonderful, that I thought I was too ... insignificant to be of any consequence in your life."
> "You are everything that matters," Rayburn said ...
> "No vote, no Act of Parliament, no alteration of a woman's status could make you more important to me than you already are just by being a woman."
> "I want to be ... your woman," Viola whispered.
> Then because she was shy she hid her face against his neck.

Cartland's version of romantic love is spiritual rather than sexual and in a message to the First Romantic Book Lovers' Conference, she openly crusaded for the exclusion of sex from romances:

> ... all decent women dislike pornography. It's degrading and humiliating and like me it makes them feel sick. To me, it's appalling that so many well known authors, especially in America, who write very well should think that sex must be included.

Cartland's books themselves constitute a series. Noted in the *Guinness Book Of Records* as the most prolific author alive, Cartland reportedly sells a million copies of every book in many countries, including North America. On the basis of her popularity alone, one can see that sexual purity still holds an appeal for many readers; however, the general trend in romance is towards more, not less sexuality.

Heroines need no longer be virgins and some series make that premise their *raison d'être*. Jove's romance series title, Second Chance, stresses the fact that the romance described in the book is not the heroine's first experience. Heroines may be widowed or divorced, implying previous sexual experience. The editorial guidelines for the Harlequin American romance series also include sexually experienced women as heroines: "She can have been married, widowed, or divorced." One must be somewhat cautious about the magnitude of such changes because these guidelines also indicate that if the heroine has never been legally married, "her previous sexual experiences need not be discussed." Read "should not be discussed"? Virginity is no longer required but sexual experience on the part of the heroine is not acceptable if it is not sanctioned by legal bonds or at least "true love."

Within these limitations, however, the diminished emphasis on virginity is paralleled by an increasing emphasis on female sexual responsiveness and physical interaction between the hero and heroine. Category romances are getting steamy. Witness the titles of three series: Candlelight's Ecstasy Romances, Silhouette's Desire Romances and Signet's Rapture Romances. Publishers have learned that sex sells and most series have deliberately moved to incorporate not only more sex scenes but also more explicit sex scenes, though they draw the line at "carnal sex." Signet's editorial guidelines for the Rapture series instruct the writer on the parameters to be followed:

> The hero and heroine will make love several times ... and the lovemaking will be described more intimately and at greater length. ... it is

important that each love scene be an integral part of the plot development.... Foreplay and afterplay, with descriptions of what the hero and heroine think and say to one another before, during, and after making love can provide this, as can a change in the setting (i.e., outside in the afternoon rather than in the bedroom at night); a switch in the seducer/seduced roles; a change in the level of experience or the attitude of one of the participants: an infinite number of distinctions can be made.

The ability to write convincing, sensual sex scenes is so crucial in modern category romances that the First Romantic Book Lovers' Conference devised a special award for the best writer of sex scenes, the Pearl Award, which went to Alice Morgan, an author in Dell's Candlelight Ecstasy series and Harlequin's American series. Here is an example of Morgan's award-winning sex from her romance, *The Sands of Malibu:*

> Carlyn arched her body toward Nick's hips, wild with the urgent need to caress him. Her nostrils flared daintily as she breathed deep of his heated skin. With eager fingers she unbuttoned his shirt and lightly ran them across his broad chest. The rapid beat of his heart inflamed her – she gloried in her effect on him. Whispering his name over and over, she felt his mouth leave her lips to plunder her neck before trailing downward to her burgeoning breasts.
>
> Nick placed his knee between her legs as his lean fingers slid the length of her body. Palms trembling at the feel of her bare thigh, he pushed her skirt aside in his quest to touch every inch of satiny leg. When his fingers touched the lace edge of her panties, he slid them under the material, his hand intimately cupping the firm smoothness of her rounded buttocks. Her slender body was supple as he drew her hips against his rock-hard flesh....
>
> His hands released her buttocks to stroke over her body to her breasts.... Her full, mature breast cupped in his palm, he lowered his face, nuzzling her low-cut bra aside to take the rosy nipple into his mouth. Her body shuddered, the enticed peak hardening and swelling to the flicking of his tongue and warmth of his mouth.[15]

The position of the hero and heroine on the book's cover is a good indication of how much sex there is in the romance. If they are not touching at all, the story does not have any detailed sex scenes. If they are touching, the degree of sexuality escalates, with different touching positions symbolizing the amount of sexual involvement: "hands above the waist innocent frolic; hands below the waist or on the breasts = sexual, prone positions = keep this one in a locked drawer."[16] The pictures also tell readers how sexually responsive and aggressive the heroine is. There are two types of embrace, the "hesitant heroine's" and the "cognizant heroine's."[17] The first kind is the more traditional portrayal of female sexuality and indicates that the hero pursues the heroine, who resists and perhaps capitulates, against her better judgment. The second kind of embrace is a departure from traditional sexual encounters and indicates that the heroine is responsive and probably even active in the pursuit of romantic-sexual gratificaton.

Artists use colours, curves and lettering to convey the degree of sensuality in the novel. Some artists and art directors have broken away from the hearts and flowers motifs used in the past to denote simple sentimental romances, in favour of complex subliminal symbols more consistent with the sexual romances. This strategy has apparently worked. Bantam's Circle of Love series, with its flower wreath design folded, while Silhouette's Desire series, which features "hot" covers, has flourished. Milt Charles, art director for Silhouette, has developed a distinctive approach to romance cover design:

> Charles maintains ... that if readers are exposed to sophisticated, innovative cover art, they will buy it – thereby raising their own art appreciation level and the standards of mass market cover art at the same time. His work is bold – sometimes brazen – with expensive printing techniques and complex combinations of Freudian, Jungian, and surrealist symbols; Katherine Hepburn-like heroines; Mannerist elongated and contorted figures; and strong color combinations that use only touches of yellow and green (what he calls the "unromantic colors").[18]

These bold covers reflect the increasingly sexual nature of the books.

The fourth area of variation in category romances is the degree of realism. Generally, categories are becoming more realistic. Not only are heroines more career-oriented but the books contain allusions to or discussions of social problems as well as the more common personal ones. This is a notable departure from the stress-free romances of the recent past, which starred heroines who were eager to chuck their typically female jobs like nursing or secretarial work in exchange for traditional marriages. Heroines may still be secretaries or nurses but they can also be police officers (author Alice Morgan is a former police officer), journalists or business managers. In addition, rather than giving up their work after marriage, some heroines now continue working, combining career aspirations and marriage.

In conjunction with this, the accident-prone bumbling of heroines that often called forth heroic rescues has been supplemented if not replaced in some cases by practicality and competence. In fact, if I had to summarize the change in heroines in one sentence, I would say they have gone from being pure and incompetent to being impure and competent.

The kinds of problems included in these modern romances range from personal troubles like unhappy childhoods or previous disastrous love affairs to social problems like political repression or ecological issues. The trend is to use "real" problems rather than the superficial conflicts based on prolonged communication problems and mistaken identities that occurred between the heroes and heroines in earlier category romances. For example, *Sea Lightning,* a 1980 Harlequin Romance by Linda Harrel, a Greenpeace supporter, is basically a "save the whales" romance. The heroine, an illustrator, is called to the coast of Argentina to work with the hero, a marine biologist, who is on a one-man crusade to save a whale breeding ground from heedless offshore oil drilling companies. *Sea Lightning* also uses personal problems as a plot device. The hero has a hostile, distant relationship with his mother who abandoned him in his youth that prevents him from trusting women in general and specifically from loving the heroine. All of these problems are resolved to some degree by the end of the novel so the stress on happy endings remains, but the fact that social and personal problems are mentioned at all is a relatively new phenomenon. Romances will never become "problem novels" or "social criticism" novels because they are read for escape and entertainment; nevertheless they are becoming more realistic.

Romance covers also reflect this change. Those series that are billed as realistic modern romances, like the Love and Life series, have substituted photographs for artistic depictions. Photographic covers can also be found in the young teen romances, which tend to be more realistic and sexually subdued than the adult series. Silhouette has used photographic covers on its First Love series as a "hook" to attract attention to the series by holding a national cover girl contest that was advertised in *Tiger Beat Star,* a Harlequin publication at the time. Pictures of the finalists appeared in the magazine and the winner was photographed for a cover of a First Love Romance.

The standard category romance has developed many new aspects. All of the new series base their individual appeals on different historical periods, ages of heroines, degrees of sexuality and degrees of realism. The most remarkable developments have been in the latter two areas. Most publishers of categories are responding to reader pressure to incorporate into their romances social changes that have evolved out of the "sexual revolution" and the women's movement.

Harlequin Enterprises has both participated in these changes and lagged behind them. It has cut back on the numbers of Harlequin Romances, its most traditional series, while increasing production of Harlequin Presents, its "racier" series. Even the regular Harlequin Romances have gotten more sexual and realistic, yet Harlequin has not made the transition as quickly or as noticeably as some other publishers. Harlequin's operating philosophy has been that "you don't change a winning ball game." Critics warn, however, that if you wait until you're losing to change your strategies, it may be too late – and Harlequin has lost ground to its competitors. Dell's Candlelight series has moved ahead with brisk sales and after two years of operations, Silhouette captured 20 percent of the romance market.[19] (Accurately calculating each company's market share is difficult because publishers inflate their claims. One industry observer has commented that if you add up all the market shares claimed by publishers, you get 150 percent.[20]) Harlequin is still the industry leader but it will have to fight harder than before to remain so.

Harlequin is attempting a comeback with its North American edited Worldwide Library series of SuperRomances, which are longer, more realistic and more sensual. Their length (380 pages) allows the writer to develop characters, subplots and story elements in more depth than any of Harlequin's shorter series. The *Romantic Times* has predicted that the new trend in romances will be suspense: "Look for a dash of 'Jane' Bond to appear, mixed with some earthy intrigue. Like 'frocks,' women don't want the same thing every year!"[21] SuperRomances have incorporated an element of suspense or adventure, which also distinguishes them from Harlequin's other series. This line has done well and Harlequin has increased the number of SuperRomances released monthly. The American series is another effort to capture the reader market that is demanding new twists in the romance formula. Also a North American edited line, it features realistic American settings and characters. Series editor Vivian Stephens has broken tradition by publishing romances with ethnically and racially diverse heroines rather than restricting the series to traditional white, Anglo-Saxon Protestant heroines. These romances are longer than the regular Harlequin Romances but shorter than the SuperRomances. Harlequin's latest offering, another North American product, is the Temptation series, an attempt to enter the market of sensuous romances.

The shift from the all-important contribution of Harlequin's Mills and Boon company to its North American branches is a reflection of the shift in the popularity of "sweet" English romances with mild heroines and small-scale action to more flamboyant American romances with assertive heroines and dramatic action. The desire for "action" was evident in the popularity of gothic romances, which sold very well in the 1960s. Gothics, which were written by both English and American authors, revolved around the heroine's fear that someone was trying to kill her. Love scenes and murder attempts were woven together in a fascinating mixture of action and inaction. Heroines were caught in the middle of life-threatening intrigue yet they were seldom able to avert their fate without the assistance of a strong male.

The gothic gave way to the predominantly American-authored "bodice ripper" in the 1970s. These books were long, sweeping historical epics in which heroines endured trials and tribulations over a span of years and continents until they finally triumphed through a combination of fortitude, intelligence and great beauty. The name "bodice ripper" was derived from the frequent rapes and sexual assaults that the heroines experienced. "Bodice-ripper" heroines were portrayed to be stronger and more active characters than gothic heroines. Editors of category romances, noting the popularity of the "bodice rippers," have borrowed the longer lengths, the overt sexuality and the assertive heroine from these romances.

Harlequin's new series are an attempt to modify its "sweet" romances with popular gothic and "bodice-ripper" elements, but these adaptions may be too late to take advantage of the brand-name loyalty that Harlequin has used to ensure sales in the past. *Forbes* predicted that: "Indeed with so many publishers entering the market, the magic of marketing brand-name books may wear off. Confronted with an excess of choice, readers may resort to buying books based on author, title, or cover."[22] Overcrowding may also lead to a decline in quality as publishers accept books they would have rejected before in a frantic attempt to increase their number of titles. Stung by some unsatisfactory romances in a series, readers then become wary and more discriminating. In addition, readers become bored with a romance formula available in such quantity, which was what eventually happened to the gothics and "bodice rippers." Although Harlequin still receives letters from women who declare their loyalty to the brand name, readers increasingly mention loyalty to specific authors as a factor in their choice of books. This means that Harlequin will have to develop followings for individual authors. In order to survive in a fiercely competitive market, they will also have to control for quality to preserve what brand-name loyalty remains and adapt more quickly to reader demands than they have in the past.

* * *

Publishers are not the only people who have profited from the romantic book boom in the last ten years. Romances have filled the coffers of a host of related support industries like bookstores and supermarkets. One distributor estimated that the space devoted to category romances in bookstores jumped 50 percent from 1981 to 1982.[23] American chains like B. Dalton and Waldenbooks have set up plexiglass romance display centres in their stores and the most popular romances invariably rank among the bookstores' most profitable titles. In fact, romance sales account for 30 percent of B. Dalton's mass market paperback sales.[24] Some independent bookstore owners have decided to specialize in romances since they have discovered that these are the books that sell. For example, Glenn Hostetter of the Book Nook in Jacksonville, Florida noted that romances constituted only 10 percent of his stock but 65 percent of his sales.[25]

Some of these specialty bookstores carry one or more of the newsletters that have sprung up to serve readers, bookstore owners and writers. Barbara Wren, a B. Dalton employee, publishes *Barbara's Critiques,* a review service that helps readers choose among the increasing numbers of romances available each month.[26] Vivian Lee Jenning's weekly newsletter, *Boy Meets Girl,* on the other hand, is aimed at industry executives who can pay the $125-a-year subscription price.[27] The biggest newsletter is Kathryn Falk's *Romantic Times,* which offers book reviews and industry gossip. Falk, author of *Love's Leading Ladies,* a collection of biographical sketches, philosophy, astrological signs and recipes of some of the best-known romantic authors, began publishing the bi-monthly, thirty-page newspaper in the summer of 1981 and it immediately flourished. A year later, the *Romantic Times* had over 12,000 subscribers with some 50,000 copies of each issue printed.[28] Falk has done much to publicize the romantic fiction industry. She and the *Romantic Times,* in conjunction with Long Island University's Brooklyn Center Institute of Continuing Education, sponsor the annual Romantic Book Lovers' Conferences, which attract considerable media attention.

The *Romantic Times* is a repository of romance writers' aids, another spin-off industry. Falk, for instance, has written a book, *How to Write a Romance and Get It Published,* which is advertised in the newspaper. Another enterprising author offers a book containing over 2,000 one-line descriptions of heartbeats, smiles, kisses and sex; another's book suggests opening and closing scenes. In addition, all of the advice sessions at the Romantic Book Lovers' Conference are taped and the cassettes made available through the newspaper, which also advertises other conferences. Obviously, romantic fiction profits are no longer the exclusive property of publishers.

Writing romances can be highly profitable for writers as well as for other industry participants. Industry reports vary, but *Forbes* is probably the most accurate in its estimate of royalty income for category romance writers:

> A first-time author who delivers an acceptable manuscript ... can expect a $6,000 advance and royalties of perhaps 8%. Nearly all titles that make it into print have a similar sales appeal, so that might work out to a gross income of $30,000. A real pro can turn out ten books annually and afford to live as well as most corporate executives.[29]

Advances, royalties and print runs vary from publisher to publisher so, for example, Harlequin has the largest print runs (500,000 copies per book) while Dell has one of the largest advances ($10,000 per book). Authors also differ in their ability to negotiate advances and royalties. Very popular writers like Janet Dailey make considerably more than 8 percent royalties, and much higher advances as well. She is also one of the most prolific writers and is consequently very wealthy, but most writers cannot turn out a book every two weeks. And, of course, the really big advances do not go to category romance writers at all. Compare the figures cited above to Avon's advance of $3.5 million to Rosemary Rogers for her next two historical romances.[30]

Neither Rogers nor Dailey is representative of romantic authors and editor Pam Strickler warns that: "'The popular notion that romance writers become rich and famous overnight is pure fantasy.'" She adds: "' ... considering the size of advances for first books, I certainly don't encourage aspiring writers to quit their jobs right away.'"[31] Nevertheless, writers who do get a first novel published with even a relatively low advance and royalty percentage have reason to feel triumphant for, like rich men trying to enter heaven, many try but few succeed. Harlequin receives over 1,000 unsolicited manuscripts a month and accepts only 1 percent of these. Some publishers do not look at unsolicited manuscripts, preferring to deal exclusively with agents' submissions.

In addition to potential income, the prospect of interesting work encourages many to take pen in hand. Just as women in the nineteenth century in England and North America turned to writing as one of the few satisfying careers open to them, women today are motivated by the same needs. For example, Elizabeth Hoy, author of over thirty Harlequins, wanted to try to write for a living because she hated being a secretary:

> It was decided that I should take a course in shorthand and typing and become a secretary, a prospect that appalled me. But I had no choice. No one believed that I would ever succeed in earning a living with my pen. As soon as I had managed to receive some kind of diploma, I worked for a time as a secretary / receptionist.... Goaded beyond endurance by this hated job, I rushed over one day to the Daily News office and demanded to be taken on the staff ...[32]

Many other romance writers, including Rosemary Rogers, Mary Burchell, Janet Dailey, Patricia Matthews and Rebecca Brandewyne, have been secretaries. (This perhaps explains why so many heroines in earlier romance fiction were secretaries.) Other writers are typically housewives, teachers or journalists in background. Although not all of the writers hate their traditional occupations, as Elizabeth Hoy did, few regret leaving them behind.

Nina Baym, author of *Woman's Fiction: A Guide To Novels By and About Women in America, 1820-1870,* indicates that during this earlier period: "Most of the American authors were middle-class women who needed money.... only middle-class women had sufficient education to know how to write books and only those who needed money attempted it."[33] Modern romance writers are also generally middle-class women who need money. One contemporary author whose life circumstances could easily have been described in Baym's book is Harlequin's Jane Donnelly, a young married woman who was suddenly widowed and forced to earn a living. Reluctant to leave her five-year-old child, she decided to try to write at home. Marion Chesney is another housewife who was thrown into a writing career by financial need. She and her husband could not pay for their son's school tuition and she could not find a job anywhere. To escape from her woes, she began reading Regency romances. One day, after reading a poorly written one, she exclaimed that she could do better than that. With her husband's encouragement, she tackled the job:

> "The time to pay the school tuition was breathing down my neck and the wolf had got its paw inside the door," Marion recalls. "I wrote the first fifty pages of *Regency Gold,* plus the plot, and sent it to the agent. She sent it to Fawcett who bought it on the spot and the advance was what I owed St. Ann's school down to the last penny."[34]

On the basis of numerous stories such as these, *Time* concluded that: "Novice authors, in fact, tend to be housewives, supplementing the family income ..."[35] Bantam Vice President Rolene Saal concurs with this statement with her vision: "' ... as the sun sets across the land, the typewriters come out and the ladies go to work.'"[36] "Supplementing" the family income may be the intent of some writers but if they succeed, many of them become the main breadwinners. In many cases, women writers are the sole source of support for themselves and their families. The term "supplementing" is reminiscent of the antiquated, inaccurate notion that women work, according to their whim, for "pin money." This is not true of women in general nor is it true of women writers.

Because of their financial success, romance writers have become very visible "Horatio Alger" figures for millions of women. They tell their rags-to-riches stories on television talk shows; they are featured in *People* magazine. Readers in every part of North America cherish the notion that, given the time and opportunity, they too could become writers. Traditionally, "Horatio Alger" stories for women have been about young, beautiful women who marry their way up the social ladder. (Indeed, this has been a theme in romantic fiction!) The new fantasy, however, features "ordinary" women, "late bloomers" and "just housewives," who work their way to the top by their own imagination, intelligence, market savvy and self-discipline. Of course, very few people can avoid poverty and boredom by becoming romance writers. Of all the women who try, only seven hundred are presently published in North America.[37] Nevertheless, it is both positive and significant that the fantasy reinforces women's achievement.

Besides the financial rewards, women writers turn to romance for emotional escape and solace. Doris E. Smith, for example, began writing when her parents died: "In 1961 I woke up and grew up. The family circle was narrowing.... The darkness of my world had somehow to be alleviated and the the only escape I possessed was writing." [38] The horrors of World War II inspired Harlequin writers Marjorie Lewty and Jean MacLeod to take refuge in their romance writing; a preoccupied husband and a difficult young child drove Brooke Hastings to reading and writing romances as a form of escape. Often housebound either through illness or mothering, isolated, and in need of a separate source of self-esteem, women writers begin their work.

Frequently, writers have to sandwich their writing in between domestic repsonsibilities. Contemporary romance authors, like Jane Austen and Kate Chopin before them, write in common living-family rooms, at the kitchen or dining-room table, subject to the multiple interruptions of family life. Lilian Peake, author of over thirty Harlequins, describes the difficulty of working in this environment:

> But it is not easy being a writer and a wife and a mother. Even when I shut myself away and start to write, I cannot leave my other roles behind. Sometimes I am just catching a thought out of the fast-flowing river of my subconscious and am about to land it in word form on the typewriter when the bedroom door bursts open and one of the family walks in. They tell me chattily about the film they have just seen on television or something someone told them that day.
>
> I make a frantic grab at my catch, but as my divided mind tries to listen intelligently to what they are saying, the thought slips through the "fingers" of my brain and is gone forever![39]

To escape the interruptions, some women work at night after everyone has gone to bed: "I used to creep downstairs at night after my husband and daughter were fast asleep and cover pages and pages of exercise books with my writing. Then at two a.m. or so, I would crawl exhausted up the stairs and fall fast asleep"[40] (Mary Wibberley). Obviously, this working arrangement has its drawbacks and must take its toll. One of the reasons that many romance writers are "late bloomers" is that they wait until after their families have grown up before they begin their careers. Over and over the women refer to the impact their family has on their work. Although it is a source of invaluable emotional support and encouragement, the family is also a major distraction:

> When the children came along, the time and the inclination to write waned steadily. Looking after three daughters was an exhausting occupation (Yvonne Whittal).[41]

> To me, writing has become a compulsion and something I enjoy, although with a relatively young family, I am unable to spend as many hours at the typewriter as I would like (Helen Bianchin).[42]

Tellingly, one of the first things that women writers do with their new-found wealth is to build a study onto their homes to which they can retreat and work in peace with the legitimacy of earned income backing up their claim to privacy.

A combination of financial and achievement needs along with the possibility of emotional escape motivates many romance writers – but why do they write romance? The answer is, most simply, that they write what they like to read. Janet Dailey, for example, says that she always knew that she wanted to be a novelist but she didn't know what kind of novels she wanted to write until she discovered Harlequins: "I became hooked on Harlequins. At some point during the next two years, the idea crystallized that this was the type of book I wanted to write."[43] The one characteristic that seems to apply to all romantic fiction writers is that they are romance *readers*. So many writers have sprung from the ranks of readers that one how-to-get-published manual advises aspiring writers to identify themselves as readers to the publisher when they submit their work.

Richard Hoggart, in his study of English working-class culture, found that popular writers typically emerged from the culture and group of people for whom they were writing and that they shared the same likes and dislikes:

They become writers ... because they can body those fantasies into stories and characters, and because they have a fluency in language. Not the attitude of language of the creative writer, trying to mould words into a shape which will bear the peculiar quality of his experience; but a fluency, a 'gift of gab', and a facility with thousands of stock phrases which will set the figures moving on the highly conventionalized stage of their readers' imaginations. They put into words, and intensify the daydreams of their readers, often with considerable technical skill. Their relation to their readers ... is more direct than that of the creative writer. They do not create an object-in-itself; they act as picture-makers for what is behind the readers' daydreams ...[43]

Although Hoggart underestimates the creativity required to write fomulaic stories, his general description of popular fiction writers does apply to romance writers. Thus, Shirley Busbee, historical romance author, declares: "My idea of heaven is a stack of Harlequins, a chaise, and a Diet Pepsi."[45]

Romantic writers are an intriguing lot because of the double message they send. Romantic fiction is beginning to be influenced by feminism in the sense that the heroines are increasingly competent, sexual human beings, yet romances still glamourize traditional values. The contradiction between writers' lives and the stories they created was more apparent in the past. Then, writers wrote exclusively about heroines who promptly abandoned their occupations upon marriage; today, the heroines, like their creators, more frequently demand both love and career. In addition, romance authors themselves are probably more traditional before they start writing romances than after they publish because the experience of fame and wealth alters them. A growing number of these women identify themselves as feminists and testify to the positive changes they have experienced:

I've become a feminist since 1977 and Rick [her husband] admires that. He's much more ready to share – housework, decisions, everything. He knows that I won't back down or take second place.... There's no telling whether these changes might have occurred anyway, without my career and success, but I do know that my financial independence makes us both take me more seriously (Cynthia Wright).[46]

It is partially due to women writers such as these that the romance formula has changed to include strong heroines. Many writers were relieved to be able to abandon frail misses in favour of colourful, active women.

Emerging from this assertiveness is also an increasing outspokenness about the romantic fiction industry and critical responses to it. Writers are attempting to organize to improve the standards within their field and to combat the negative image of romance in the literary world. Several authors in Kathryn Falk's *Love's Leading Ladies* lambast narrow-minded critics of romance and, with a savvy born of experience and financial success, remind the publishing industry of its dependence upon their labours and the romance genre itself. Falk also feels strongly about the unfavourable literary reception of romances and devised a critics award, presented at the 1982 Romantic Book Lovers' Conference to Ray Walters of the *New York Times* for his coverage of the genre at a time when few critics took romance seriously. These efforts are evidence of a new sense of professionalism among romance writers.

* * *

At the beginning of the 1980s, Harlequin Enterprises faced intense competition where once they reigned unchallenged; flourishing romance writers learned to see romance as a business proposition as well as an entertaining pastime; and romances started to incorporate some of the social changes evolving from women's increased economic independence, the "sexual revolution" and the women's movement. Why did all these changes occur when they did? Women readers' overwhelmingly positive response to Harlequin's romances began the chain of events. Harlequin's sales and profits in turn attracted other publishers into the market. Like any company that makes its sales pitch by claiming that its product is "new and improved," the publishers entering the market tried to find a new angle on romance. Editors were given more leeway and writers "bloomed" under the loosened guidelines. The industry is more experimental now than ever before. Despite these alterations, however, romances are still formula fiction. Chapter Four looks at the parameters of that formula by outlining the basic plot and typical cast of characters in a Harlequin romance.

*

CHAPTER FOUR

THE ROMANCE FORMULA

She closed her eyes and let her thoughts rove deliciously. To be married to someone tall and dark and masterful, and to return from a honeymoon to this house in the sun. A lovely home, a husband, children.... Heavens, how trite could one get!

A Summer at Barbazon
Kathryn Blair

Nothing produces such an effect as a good platitude.

Oscar Wilde

Some Harlequin representatives deny that Harlequins are formula fiction. Fred Kerner, for example, maintains that each romance is distinct and moreover, that romance readers are appreciative of the books' variety. Harlequin keeps short plot summaries of all its romances and checks each manuscript to ensure it is not too similar to ones already published. Otherwise, Kerner says, Harlequin would be bombarded with complaints from attentive readers.

There are differences between the books, of course. For example, Violet Winspear creates particularly exotic characters; each one of Janet Dailey's American romances is set in a different state of the union; Marjorie Norrel writes only nurse-doctor romances. However, these differences revolve around character descriptions, settings or minor plot mechanisms – the plot structure in all of them is essentially the same. Harlequin's defence of its romances is quixotic, given the evidence that not only analysts but readers can easily recognize the formulaic structure of the novels. One reader I interviewed commented:

They're all the same. They really are. You know the girl's hair colour is different, and they'll describe each one in detail and the names will be different but each story is the same. That's all there is to it.

The basic plot is that the hero and heroine meet and fall in love but there is an obstacle to their love. In this, Harlequins conform to many classic tales of romantic love in which the lovers are constantly stymied by insurmountable obstacles – for example, Tristan and Isolde, Orpheus and Eurydice, Romeo and Juliet. Love is denied by death in these stories but Harlequins, like most contemporary formula fiction, always feature a happy ending. Sometimes the great mimetic romances of the past are adopted by Harlequin writers, who rewrite the objectionable tragic endings. Thus the back cover of *Clouded Waters* by Sue Peters proclaims:

The feud between the Montagues and the Capulets was like a childish squabble compared to the long-standing quarrel between the Dane and Baird families. It had already ruined the romance between Marian Dane and Adam Baird. But now Fate had brought them together again. Were they being offered a second chance?[1]

Of course they were. Romeo and Juliet may perish but Adam and Marian will live happily ever after. In Harlequins the obstacle is only temporary or even chimeric. The barriers are removed in the last chapter and the hero and the heroine are allowed to unite. Any variation unfolds itself within this structure.

Lack of communication is the basis of most obstacles between the hero and heroine. The most common version of this communication gap involves rival men and women who vie for the love of the heroine and hero. In these plots the heroine and/or hero believes that the other is in love with a rival. They try to fight their growing attraction to each other but their attempts are unsuccessful, which fortunately does not matter because their belief is unfounded. For example, the heroine in *Golden Harvest* by Stella Frances Nel falsely assumes the hero is married so when he kisses her, she thinks he is a "philanderer." When this misunderstanding is finally cleared up, she confesses:

I've loved you from the time I met you, so you might as well know. Even when I thought you were married. My mind was disgusted, but my heart was irrevocably yours![2]

There are other misunderstandings, such as noble or innocent actions on the part of the hero or heroine that are wrongly perceived by or maliciously interpreted to the loved one by less noble and innocent people (usually the rivals). For example, in *Dark Viking* by Mary Wibberley, the hero suspects the heroine is a foreign spy who is interested in the Early Warning System that protects America and Western NATO powers from sudden missile attacks from the East. Instead she is a weary model on holidays and interested only in him. A little trust and communication resolve this problem.

Other obstacles that are based on more concrete problems are also resolved. These difficulties include age differences, pressing family responsibilities, conflicting loyalties or, occasionally, social class differences. By the end of the story, however, these difficulties have either been redefined as unimportant or the hindering conditions have changed. For example, an overly young heroine is suddenly matured by her love for the hero or a heroine's dependent, crippled younger sister miraculously walks and gets married, freeing the heroine to marry as well.

There is a trend towards incorporating more realistic obstacles and problems, particularly in Harlequin's SuperRomance and American Romance series. Increasingly, instead of mere mistaken identities and lack of communication, heroines and heroes are likely to have serious social and psychological reasons to distrust not only the loved one but the emotional state of love and the institution of marriage. Romances published in the last few years now use generalized gender antagonism (he is suspicious of all women; she hates all men) as an obstacle between the two main protagonists. This reference to "the battle between the sexes" is a departure from the earlier standard assumption of complete harmony and complementarity. There was conflict between individual men and women but never this overt questioning of the relationship between the sexes or discussion of issues like child custody and sexual violence. Social problems such as political repression and ecological destruction are also entering the novels, sometimes as the issue that unites the hero and heroine, sometimes as the barrier dividing them. Yet even these new obstacles are alleviated or eradicated. Harlequins have retained the happy ending.

The combined emphasis on problems and their inevitable resolution conveys the general tone of optimism that characterizes Harlequins. In earlier Harlequins, this tone was one of optimistic fatalism.

The message was that one does not have much control over one's life but things usually work out for the best. Authors occasionally used fate to foretell significant events and to build anticipation. For example:

> Then why on earth should he have this premonition ... that here something more important, more dramatic than anything he had yet experienced, was going to happen? Because sheer chance had brought him, and when that happened, one never knew whether, actually it was not chance at all? Mark shrugged his shoulders. He was something of a fatalist. What would be, would be. There was nothing one could do about it.[3]

In other instances fate was used to technically justify unlikely coincidences. In Elizabeth Hoy's *Into a Golden Land*, the heroine's father gets a job offer in Algeria just when he wants to go to a warm climate to recover from the flu. The heroine goes with him to keep house and discovers her love of two years before, working for the same Sheik as her father. Even the characters' credulities are strained by this as they remark:

> "You and I landing up in this oriental set-up, Young Warrender! I just can't believe it. The long arm of coincidence stretching to a breaking point."
> "It is rather extraordinary," Allison agreed drily.

This is explained and justified by fate:

> And fate had brought her all the way to Sidi bou Kef to find him again. It was like a beautiful shining pattern falling into place.[4]

The optimistic fatalism that once prevailed unchallenged in Harlequin Romances has been shaken by two sources of doubt that have emerged in recent romances. The first modification is the growing recognition that fate is not as benign as it was portrayed to be in earlier romances. For example, in *The Man She Married* by Violet Winspear, fate is described in ominous terms: "Dark ... dark like fate which always waited a few steps ahead of everyone's hopes and expectations. A dream could be glimpsed, the future planned, but there was no guarantee that the dream would become a reality."[5] This ominous note is consistent with the incorporation of more serious problems and elements of realism into the romances. It is also consistent with the hard economic times and violence of recent years that present a threat that cannot be ignored even in light fantasy fiction. This intrusion of reality is thrust into the background, however, by Harlequins' guarantee that, for heroines at least, the dream will come true. The second modification is the awareness slowly permeating the romances that people construct their fates by their own actions. In Charlotte Lamb's *Desire,* the heroine realizes that: "There was only pointless futility in quarreling with fate. Fate in this case was only another name for her own folly."[6] Dropping the emphasis on fate as the main determinant of one's life is a positive change that stems from the growth of heroines into more assertive, competent women than they have been in the past. Nevertheless, this new focus on individual responsibility stops short of the recognition that social institutions such as corporations or governments shape people's lives. The realism that characterizes recent Harlequins occurs primarily in the personal and emotional realms and fails to confront wider social and political issues.

Even with the decreased use of fate as a motif, romances still stress optimistic fatalism more than do other forms of formula fiction, particularly those forms read by men. The happy ending is a standard feature of almost all light fiction but in adventure and western stories, male characters are active in their pursuit of that happpy ending. They earn their happiness; they do not wait around for fate to intervene. Why is there a more frequent use of fate in romances? Frank Parkin argues that a belief in fate stems from social and political inequality:

> The interpretation of social reality in terms of chance happenings and the mysterious intervention of fate is common among groups of strata whose members have little direct control over their environment.... The underclass in any stratified order is much more likely to be at the receiving end of other men's decisions. It is not too surprising that those who are less active than acted upon should be prone to view the social world as one governed by apparently irrational forces beyond their control.[7]

Although the term "men" in the quotation cited above is probably intended to mean people, this is a case where the word is more usefully read to mean males. Women have been relatively powerless in our society, on the receiving end of decisions made by men in their positions as heads of governments and heads of families. Traditionally more acted upon than active in controlling their lives, women often fall back on fate or luck to explain significant events in their social world.

***

The basic plot and the optimistic tone are relatively fixed features of Harlequins. In contrast, the setting is one of the most flexible elements in the formula. It is also one of the least important elements, because the setting is ultimately reduced to providing the background for the real focus of the story, which is the romance. After all, one can fall desperately in love anywhere in the world, whether it be under an apple tree in North America or a palm tree in Africa.

The setting contributes ambience and Harlequin emphasizes it in its advertisements: "You'll be swept to distant lands you've dreamed of visiting.... You'll come to know them so well, you'll feel like you've lived there!" Back cover "grabbers" and cover illustrations usually draw attention to the setting. For example, the cover of *Desert Doctor* by Violet Winspear shows the hero wearing traditional Moroccan headgear and the heroine racing across the desert on horseback while the back cover says: "The very air of magical Morocco breathed romance, instilling thoughts of love into every heart..."

The amount of scenery description varies with the specific book, author and series (the Harlequin Romance series has more non-romance detail than the Harlequin Presents series, which focuses on the love relationship), but in almost every novel there is some general description. The following passage, a typical one, touches upon most of the elements usually described:

> Time passed; the fleeting twilight shades of gold and orange and rust melted into the deep purple of night. Stars appeared, hanging like diamonds suspended beneath a canopy of softest tulle. A wisp of cloud here and there, a floating moon, the calm dark sea, and carried on the breeze a scent of roses and jasmine. Sheep bells on the mountainside, a distant bray of a donkey.... This was Cyprus, island in the sun.[8]

Sometimes Harlequins contain an elaborate cataloging of the area's flora and fauna. For example, in Essie Summers' *Through All the Years,* the reader is told about no less than twenty-five types of flowers, shrubs and trees! Many readers probably skip or skim the details to get on with the story. One reader comments: "It's nice to read and learn about other countries, but a little less scenery and more romance wouldn't come amiss."[9] Most Harlequins, however, are not so detailed and would not call forth protest. Authors are usually content to evoke the appropriate atmosphere with a few stock phrases and images. Romantic wisps of clouds and floating moons appear in Corfu, South Africa, England and Canada. Only names and temperatures change. As a result, the settings as well as the plots give only the illusion of diversity.

No matter how little or how much description of the setting is included, it must be "accurate," according to editorial policy. However, the accuracy of the descriptions of countries written about in Harlequins has been primarily limited to geographical details, not social relationships, which are potentially more controversial. This is particularly evident in earlier Harlequins set in countries like South Africa. Racial inequality, the economic exploitation of the country's raw resources by industrial nations, and political repression were ignored in favour of "happier" subjects such as sunshine, natives "born with rhythm in their bones,"[10] and benevolent whites. In these romances, blacks were reduced to objects that added local "colour" to the stories. There was a continual emphasis on physical features such as their "wide, sugar-white grins," their "rolling velvety eyes" and their "wooly-heads." They spoke in "pidgin English," and addressed their white employers as "Missy," "Bwana" or "Memasabib." They, in turn, were referred to as "boys."[11] They smelled, shuffled, were intuitively wise, simple, happy and unquestioningly loyal to their employers who were, in contrast, cultured, properous and virtuous:

> The Pearces, of course, lived in Salisbury's most select suburb.... They had a swimming pool and a tennis court, they owned stables out of town and three cars. They entertained a good deal, kept open house ...; they gave freely to charity and democratically had friends in all walks of life.[12]

Harlequin Enterprises' emphasis on providing stress-free entertainment for women readers as well as its authors' own race and class biases led to these highly romanticized, inaccurate versions of reality. More recent Harlequins are not so overtly racist or unrealistic in their depictions of race, sex and class relationships. In fact, a few new romances like *Season of Storm* by Alexandra Sellars, a 1983 Super-Romance, are strongly critical of racial injustice. The hero of *Season of Storm*, is a Native who is fighting the Canadian government and a logging company for the restoration of his tribe's land rights. The book refers to ruthless corporate policies that place profits before people, to the short life span of Native people, to the police state mentality of the RCMP and to the pervasive racism that even the heroine is forced to acknowledge is part of her and her society. The emphasis that these exploitive relationships receive in this particular book is exceptional; Harlequins generally steer a middle course between overt racism and strong opposition to racism.

Im most books, the hero and heroine are "liberal" in their attitudes about race. Racism is portrayed to be neither "nice," as befits a heroine nor "manly," as befits a hero; that's about the limit of most Harlequins' opposition to racial inequality. Generally, Harlequins try to avoid depicting the "unpleasantness" of racial inequality in the countries in which the romances are set in favour of safe, sensuous or amusing descriptions of scenery and the "quaint" customs of the locals.

Readers say they like the bits and pieces of information that are woven into the romances: "I spend many enjoyable hours reading the excellent books: learning about the culture, customs and productivity of the locale in the story."[13] Some women are even encouraged to go beyond reading the romances in more active pursuit of learning about other countries:

> I appreciate them for the delightful armchair traveling they afford. I have nearly worn out a geographic map of the British Isles looking for locations of stories and also use encyclopedia maps of the countries mentioned in the stories.

> Our first overseas visit was enriched this year by reading about various areas and cities in your books and magazines. Indeed I was anxious to see places I'd never given much thought to before![14]

Most readers, however, are content with the superficial, glamourized version of armchair travel that Harlequins offer.

Leslie Fiedler, author of *Love and Death in the American Novel*, comments on the role of exciting settings in romance:

> Action itself becomes the end, the evasion of ennui is sought through a constant change of tempo and place. Though certain landscapes ... come to have symbolic overtones, they are chiefly prized as examples of hitherto unexplored settings, glimpses of the unknown. Vicarious tourism draws the reader on.[15]

"The evasion of ennui" is what formula fiction is all about and the settings in Harlequins provide part of the safe but exciting distraction that readers seek in romance.

***

The landscape in Harlequins is peopled by two main characters, the hero and the heroine. A book usually begins by introducing the heroine and she is seldom absent from the action throughout the book. Within the first two chapters, the hero also enters the picture. The reader can easily recognize both of these characters. One might expect this to be true of the heroine but more surprisingly there is equally little suspense about the identity of the hero. They can be recognized by the descriptions of their appearance, personality and socioeconomic characteristics as well as by the amount of detail and space devoted to them. Besides these two main characters are two other important though less developed characters, the rival man and woman. Most Harlequins have at least one rival character.

The main focus of attention is on the heroine, whose appearance, personality, socioeconomic background, thoughts, emotions and even bodily sensations are described in detail. The heroine is the character with whom readers are expected to identify, no matter how different she or her experiences may be from themselves and their lives. Great care is taken to make her a fully drawn and sympathetic character.

Heroines vary in appearance from plainly attractive to beautiful. No one is ever ugly, homely or just plain. When an author is being "critical" of a heroine's appearance, she may indicate that the heroine's nose is a little too small or her mouth a little too generous for ideal beauty (never the reverse) or she may say that the heroine does not have a very conspicuous face but add that she has gold highlights in her hair, wide hazel eyes, and neat, pretty hands and feet, so the overall impression is still favourable and even glamourized.

Eyes and hair are particularly emphasized. Heroines usually have large, thickly fringed eyes of wonderful colours – dark, smoky blue; gold-green; pansy brown; or blue-violet. They also have glorious hair of varying lengths and styles but always silver-pale; thick chestnut gold; supple honey-bright blonde; or molten red-gold. Usually height and body size are also mentioned. Heroines can be either tall or short but they are inevitably slender and soft. Generally, heroines are not ravishing goddesses but they are attractive and their attractiveness is based on solid, wholesome grounds: (soft) hair, (small) bones, (soft) skin and (small) teeth.

Until the American Romance series was initiated, heroines were always White Anglo-Saxon Protestants. Vivian Stephens, the Black woman who is the editor of Harlequin's American series, is occasionally breaking away from this rigid model to publish romances with a minority heroine, but the vast majority of Harlequin romances still feature the traditionally young, pretty, White woman. This heroine reproduces the airbrushed Anglo ideal of feminine beauty that is held up to women for emulation in our society. The new Harlequin heroine is akin, in appearance and style, to the "new women" in *Cosmopolitan* and *Playboy* who radiate wholesomeness and sexuality, who speak of devoting themselves to both personal relationships and careers, and who generally present themselves as being free from all social constraints even as they conform to them. Through these portrayals, women are faced with rising expectations about what they must be and what they must look like. New demands to successfully manage both a happy family and a challenging career are placed on top of old demands to be physically attractive. Social approval for female achievement and intelligence that is emerging in Harlequins is obviously desirable but when it is not accompanied by a corresponding decrease in emphasis on female beauty, women can only experience these two combined expectations as a burden.

Ironically, even though the reader and the hero can recognize the heroine's prettiness, she is usually unaware of her attractiveness. She compares herself unfavourably to the rival woman who is everything in appearance that the heroine is not but wishes to be. If the heroine is petite, the rival woman is gracefully tall; if the heroine is tall, the rival woman is daintily petite. Harlequins capture feminine insecurity about appearance in their portrayals of heroines, creating a bond of sympathy between the heroine and the reader.

The Harlequin heroine's kind of beauty is not just skin deep; it radiates from within, for the heroine's personality matches her appearance. The most outstanding character traits of a heroine are her warmth, compassion and generosity. Heroines are loving people who often care more about others than they do about themselves:

> Here ... was love, devotion, loyalty, all the womanly virtues as well as
> the beauty of heart, mind, and character which enhances the beauties
> of physical charms and which outlasts them through all the years
> which lay ahead.[16]

This Harlequin was published in 1966 and readers will not find these sentiments expressed in the same staid style in contemporary romances, but the sentiments themselves have remained. Consider the following passage from a Harlequin Presents published in 1982:

> "Rad ... Rad!" It was a threnody of joy. "I'm glad I was able to give you so much."
> "So much and so much, my darling." He held her very close. "You're perfect. You give all the time, and it makes you so strong and sure and generous ... all woman. My woman."[17]

Passion has replaced stuffiness but that's about the only difference.

Heroines are also honest, sincere, pure and innocent. They are sometimes so open and ingenuous that they are described as being "transparently honest." Heroes' minds are impenetrable to the heroines but heroes are able to read the heroines' every thought. This is an ambiguous situation for a heroine because, while she appreciates having a person who understands what she is thinking or feeling, she is at a disadvantage because the hero's knowledge is a form of power that she does not share. She cannot reciprocate, which leaves her indebted to him. Her innocence is also problematic for the heroine because of the fine line between naiveté and gullibility. If her warmth leads her to love the hero, her naiveté jeopardizes their relationship because she temporarily believes every preposterous lie about the hero that the rivals can concoct.

Heroines may display other traits like good humour, common sense, courage, resourcefulness, modesty and sentimentality. Basically, their perceptions of people and events and their subsequent responses are based on emotion rather than reason but these emotions are generally portrayed to be valuable and good, if misguided. (The problem of misguided good intentions is worked out in the romance by the end of the book when the heroine has either learned from her mistakes or the hero provides necessary guidance – his voice of reason counterbalances her emotion.)

These predominant traits are constant but the heroine's temperament varies. Heroines can be fiery, spirited and passionate or serene, reserved and gentle. The reserved heroine is almost a thing of the past, as the new romances nearly always feature "spirited" heroines. One reason for this is that the novel is more suspenseful the more conflict there is between the hero and heroine. Another reason is that the romance industry seems to be finally responding to the women's movement by incorporating stronger heroines. One can see this in the two quotations cited earlier about the generosity and warmth of the heroines. Although the traditional image is sustained, the more recent description emphasizes the heroine's strength. Her generosity does not make her a weak, exploited person but a person who is strong and sure and "all woman." There was a time when those terms would have been contradictory rather than compatible. Of course, heroines are still not ideal role models; one seventy-five-year-old reader told me that she wished a particular heroine had "more gumption," a comment that too frequently applies to heroines. Nevertheless, there is some evidence of change for the better.

As noted in Chapter Two, heroines are relatively young, although in recent years they have been getting slightly older. The teenage heroines who used to appear in the Harlequin series have been largely displaced to the teenage romance lines. Most current heroines are in their early to mid twenties, and Harlequin's American series has no heroine younger than twenty-six.

The marital status and sexual experience of heroines are also undergoing alterations. Formerly heroines were single virgins, but this is no longer exclusively the case. A recent Harlequin Presents features a heroine who is a never-married single mother; other recent heroines are widowed, separated or divorced. Increasingly heroines who are virgins at the beginning of the romance experience sexual intercourse by the end of the romance, either within or outside the bonds of marriage. Sexual intercourse is frequently described in recent books, in contrast to the romances published ten years ago, which culminated in a chaste kiss on the final page. In many cases but not always, the heroine's previous marital and sexual experience has been with the hero, who comes back into her life.

The move towards incorporating more serious problems and realism into the plots has allowed authors to portray unhappy former marriages and sexual experiences with others. These new heroines and their frequently failed relationships inject an element of doubt into the happy ending that has always been an essential part of romances. To a great extent, the successful portrayal of a heroine today depends on the author's ability to balance the tension between the character's past experiences and her optimism for the future.

The nationality of the heroines is also changing as Harlequin pub-lishes more North American authors. Earlier heroines were predom-inantly English, a few from Commonwealth countries like Australia. There are now more North American heroines found in the romances of Canadian writers like Flora Kidd, Linda Harrel, Sandra Field and Elizabeth Graham, and American writers such as Janet Dailey. Regardless of nationality, heroines often are not on their home turf, in contrast to the heroes who usually are. This situation makes the hero appear very powerful, especially in relation to the heroine who, set down in an unknown culture or environment, is vulnerable. The heroine is frequently forced to be dependent for social or physical survival on the hero, a state of affairs which acts as a barrier between them even as it forces them together. This forced contact brings tension to the romances, a tension that is heightened by the heroine's freedom to experiment with sex away from her fam-ily, friends and coworkers, who inhibit her behaviour on her own home ground. The hero is "foreign" to her, either in nationality or personality, and he represents the lure of the forbidden in matters of sexuality.

Two other aspects of heroine's lives that are changing are educa-tional levels and occupations. In Harlequins published ten or fifteen years ago, most heroines were high-school graduates; about a third of them had post-high school, non-university education like nurse's training or secretarial school. Recent heroines are more likely to have attended college although educational levels are still not mentioned for many. In general, educational level is not considered to be an aspect of the heroine's life that the reader must know about in order to understand her. When the reader is informed about her education, it is usually in connection with her occupation. Heroines in earlier Harlequins had traditionally feminine sex-typed occupations. Nurses, predominating in the 1950s and early 1960s, were replaced by secretaries in the 1970s and the secretaries have, in turn, been sup-planted by a more diverse group of heroines in the 1980s. Journalists are very popular but one can also find storekeepers, musical per-formers, filmmakers, university research assistants, advertising copywriters and story illustrators, as well as the more traditional secretaries and models. Heroines are also bringing a new attitude to work. None of the earlier heroines planned to keep working after they were married; the reverse was almost always true. Heroes informed their prospective brides that they had no intention of letting them work; rather than challenge this domineering assertion, heroines merely beamed up at the heroes and snuggled closer. This scenario still gets played out, but far less often. Nowadays some heroines intend to keep their jobs and develop their careers after marriage but notably this usually involves freelance work that they can do at home.

At the beginning of the stories, heroines are "neither rich nor poor." They support themselves on their salaries, live in rented apartments and own a car, but that's about it in terms of property ownership or wealth. Heroines will be loved for themselves alone. By the end of the stories, they are not only loved but frequently upwardly mobile, because of their marriages or impending marriages to the heroes, who are almost always in superior social positions.

Of all the characters, heroines have the most family mentioned in the novels but a good many of them are relatively alone. At least a third of the heroines are orphans. Part of the reason for this is that the novels are quite short and there is little time to describe family relationships. In addition, the presence of a family puts the damper on the passionate interaction between the hero and the heroine. Heroines do have some support networks available to them through friends. There are an increasing number of portrayals of good, strong, caring friendships between women, in contrast to earlier Harlequins in which women friends or family members were not to be trusted because they were often rivals for the hero's love. Friends are not enough, however, and the heroines are lonely for a male lover.

Perhaps the heroines as characters can best be understood and summarized by a composite picture. The Harlequin heroine is an average woman. She is not a raving beauty but she has some good features which make her attractive. This attractiveness is reinforced by her personality because she is a nice person, kind and loving, responsible and trustworthy, although she is not perfect by any means. She has bouts of temper or irrationality but these failings can be forgiven because of her good intentions. She is working class or middle class with at least a high-school education and increasingly some form of higher education. Her occupation may vary although it is usually based upon nurturing skills or artistic ability, both acceptable feminine accomplishments. She is relatively comfortable but "missing something" in her life, which the hero will supply.

Harlequin heroines are a variation and continuation of a long tradition of fictional female characters. Margaret Dalziel, in a study of popular literature of the mid-nineteenth century, described the typical heroine in these books:

> Young and lovely, religious, submissive and dependent, confiding and sensitive and chaste, accepting without question the destiny of marriage, the heroine emerges from the pages of the popular novels and periodicals as a well understood and consistent type.[18]

Other studies of contemporary heroines have discovered the persistence of this feminine character in gothic romances, love comics, mass periodical fiction and confession magazines.[19] Part of the durability of the heroine just described is that she is a character with whom readers can easily identify for "she is at the same time like all other girls yet like all other girls want to be."[20] John Cawelti maintains that the identification of the reader with the main character is a crucial aspect of formula fiction:

> Its purpose is not to make me confront motives and experiences in myself that I might prefer to ignore but to take me out of myself by confirming an idealized self-image.... The art of formulaic character creation requires the establishment of some direct bond between us and a superior figure ...[21]

The bond between character and reader has lead to some of the changes we are now seeing in romance heroines. Readers can no longer identify with an overtly simple, religious, submissive, dependent, chaste heroine. There is still much that is traditional about a Harlequin heroine but this formulaic character is being modified to fit society's new ideal female.

***

Harlequin heroines meet their match in the hero. Readers are well informed about the hero although they are not made familiar with his every thought or emotion unless he verbalizes them himself. (This does not happen very often but it is more frequent now than in earlier Harlequins.)

Heroes have a commanding physical presence. They are invariably tall and strong; there are no short, weak heroes. Just as everything about a heroine is small, soft or slender, so everything about a hero is big, hard and strong. He is usually ruggedly handsome or just rugged. Some heroes have badly scarred faces or are crippled, or blind, but even they are strong and physically compelling. (One hardly need add that there are no equivalent heroines.)

Heroes have equally imposing personalities for they are supremely self-confident – indeed, arrogant – and accomplished. One hero, who is described as being "competence itself," has an absolute knowledge of his large corporation, is an excellent dancer, a good horseman, bilingual, a fashion expert and a wonderful lover. His competence, however, is overshadowed by another hero who is a brilliant barrister, captain of a cricket team, a beautiful diver, an expert swimmer, the perfect host, a first-class tennis player, an accomplished horseman, a delightful piano player with a great sense of rhythm, a polo player – who, to round out his talents, studies history in his spare time. Such heroes may perhaps be excused a touch of arrogance!

Heroes combine ruthlessness and drive with kindness and tenderness. They are "men of steel and velvet." At first they appear to be insensitive and unfeeling but they are capable of strong emotion once they let go of their "iron control," although this vented passion can be as violent as it is tender. An emerging trait in Harlequin heroes is their vulnerability. Heroines are increasingly aware of their ability to hurt the hero's feelings and many books now refer to the hero's pain when the heroine says something cutting to him.

Flamboyant heroes are paired with temperamental, spirited heroines. Sparks fly in their encounters and a fair amount of the plot revolves around resolving their personality clashes. By the end of the romance, the hero and heroine are completely compatible. In earlier romances there were a minority of heroes who were nice, even-tempered, innocuous men but they have nearly disappeared. The mild-mannered heroes were paired with the sweet heroines. When the heroines began to change into stronger characters, the heroes had to change as well. As one reader pointed out to me, strong-willed women intimidate most men. To make the story believable, heroes had to at least match the heroines in strength. Current heroes are authoritative, determined, capable of tenderness, urbane, passionate, proud, just, charming over-achievers. They are heroes, literally and figuratively larger than life.

Heroes are always older than heroines by at least four or as much as twenty years, with the average hero being about twelve years older than the heroine. Heroes range in age from twenty-six to forty and most of them are in their mid to late thirties. As such, they are the oldest and most experienced of the main characters. Certainly they are sexually experienced although most of them are unmarried at the time of the story. They have had affairs or they have been previously married and are widowed or divorced. Many of the formerly married heroes have a child. (An interesting pattern is that if the hero or the heroine has a child, it is usually a boy. When the heroine is the single parent, there is always a discussion about the necessity of providing her son with a father and the boy himself is instantly drawn to the hero, sometimes rather callously rejecting or ignoring his mother in the process. This emphasis on sons and the importance of providing sons with fathers is unfortunate, illustrating society's preference for sons over daughters and reinforcing the erroneous assumption that single mothers cannot raise boys to be psychologically healthy adult males. There is no comparable questioning of the parenting abilities of single fathers in Harlequins.)

Heroes are predominantly upper class, with a few falling into the upper middle class. There are no working-class heroes. Cawelti argues this is consistent with our social values. Formula fiction must be tied to contemporary culture to be effective: "One cannot write a successful adventure story about a social character type that a culture cannot conceive in heroic terms: this is why we have so few adventure stories about plumbers, janitors, or streetsweepers."[22] There are no romances about plumbers, janitors or streetsweepers. Heroes range from multinational corporation owners to self-employed professionals. If a hero is employed by others he is involved in top management and is portrayed to have complete job autonomy. He is so competent that he is free to choose where and for whom he will work, or he has the option of setting up his own business. Heroes are seldom accountable to anyone but themselves though they may be responsible for the welfare of large numbers of employees. There is a big difference, however, between "being responsible for" and "being responsible to."

The hero's high status, sense of responsibility and independence are absolutely essential in Harlequins. For example, the back cover of Anne Weale's *A Touch of the Devil,* published in a Harlequin Presents edition in 1982, reads:

> Bianca had never felt such a strong attraction to a man before. Yet Joe Crawford, the darkly handsome piano player at the local restaurant, was clearly not good husband material.
>
> Living on his boat in the small Spanish harbor, Joe would no doubt drift out of her life as he'd drifted into it. "I want you very much; come live with me," was his only offer. Could Bianca be faulted for refusing?

Joe Crawford is not "good husband material" because he is apparently an impoverished drifter. In fact Bianca does decide to take the risk and live with him but before she can take this drastic step, he is called away to his ailing grandfather's side. When they do finally get together, he proposes and she discovers that he is the heir apparent to the fourth largest privately owned company in Britain. Piano playing was merely a brief successful rebellion against his family to establish his autonomy.

Vivian Stephens, one of the most innovative editors in the business, who is in charge of Harlequin's American series, has altered some qualities in the hero:

> Hero –
> Who should be a mature American Male of any age compatable [sic] with that of the heroine. (That means younger than she or older or whatever.) He should be an achiever and upwardly mobile in his job. He does not have to own the company he works for nor does he have to be rich. He should typify the average American male. He *does not* have to be tall, dark, and handsome. He should be attractive in some way to appeal to and attract the heroine.

The Harlequin hero was never before an "average male" so these guidelines continue the trend towards more realism in romances. Yet, in spite of the modifications, the portrait of the hero retains an emphasis on occupational success and upward mobility.

This hero, like the heroine, is the result both of a literary tradition and of our society's values. The Harlequin hero still shares many of the qualities that Dalziel indicates were typical of the hero of nineteenth-century popular fiction. One need only think of Darcy in Jane Austen's *Pride and Prejudice* to realize the continuity of the wealthy, aloof yet passionate hero. This kind of hero is also consistent with a male sex-role stereotype that is a widely held ideal. Deborah David and Robert Brannon argue that there are four themes or dimensions that comprise the male sex role as we know it:

1. No Sissy Stuff: The stigma of all stereotyped feminine characteristics and qualities, including openness and vulnerability.

2. The Big Wheel: Success, status, and the need to be looked up to.

3. The Sturdy Oak: A manly air of toughness, confidence, and self-reliance.

4. Give 'Em Hell!: The aura of aggression, violence, and daring.[23]

These are all characteristics that the Harlequin hero possesses to varying degrees. However, like the changes in the makeup of the heroine in response to women's increased economic and sexual independence, the hero is being modified in accordance with men's corresponding awareness of the unrealistic demands placed on them by sex roles. The major change is that vulnerability and emotion are "in" for today's hero as long as he conforms in no uncertain way to the rest of the traditional male sex role.

Rival men and women act as foils to the hero and heroine, who exemplify the ideal man and woman. When we examine the rival characters, we learn what not to be. The rival woman, for example, is usually the villain in the romance. Unlike the heroines, rival women are portrayed to be basically evil people. At best they are self-centred and thoroughly spoiled; at worst they are mercenary, cold, aggressive bitches who will stop at nothing, including blackmail and possibly murder, to get the hero. These traits are the rival woman's true personality but this side of her is revealed only to the heroine and reader. On the surface the rival woman may appear to be charming, warm and sophisticated. This is the side that the hero is allowed to see unless her poise slips at the end in her frustration at not winning him. Then she may reveal herself to be the shallow, vicious person she actually is. Occasionally there is a nice rival woman in which case the heroine has some hesitations about "stealing" the hero away from her, but the nasty rival is the norm. For the reader of escape fiction, vanquishing a villain is more emotionally satisfying than hurting a friend.

Compared to the heroine, the rival woman is usually more beautiful, older, more sophisticated, wealthier and more sexually aggressive. In all of these respects, she is a "better match" for the hero than the heroine, yet she fails to win him. The standard interpretation of this portrayal argues that the rival woman is a negative role model that provides reinforcement for the traditional female sex role. The rival woman is seen as a sex-role rebel who breaks out of socially sanctioned female subservience to wield the power she has at her disposal as a result of her beauty, wealth and sexuality. She is punished for her rebellion by the hero's rejection of her and his choice of the more docile heroine. This interpretation is not without merit. One of the main reasons the rival woman loses the hero is that, although she is qualified in every other way, she is not nice. Being nice is a traditional female sex-role proscription and the portrayal of the rival woman's punishment for breaking this rule does reinforce the sex role.

Nevertheless it is a mistake to see the rival woman only as or even primarily as a sex-role rebel. She has more sources of power than the heroine but she does not use her power to attack traditional notions of femininity. To the contrary, she is more traditional in her behaviour and attitudes than the heroine. Rather than use her power to establish her independence, to pursue meaningful work and to establish strong support networks with other women, she directs all her energies into capturing a wealthy, prestigious male. She is willing to abdicate all her power in exchange for a man and a traditional marriage. She has no career commitment other than the pursuit of the hero: she is described as being "a man's woman" because she caters to men; she does not like other women. The negative portrayal of her character, which incorporates the most personally and socially destructive aspects of the traditional sex role, can therefore be read as a criticism of the sex role rather than a defence of it.

The despicable rival woman has her predecessors in fiction. One may recall that Jane Eyre wins Mr. Rochester away from an aristocratic, patronising beauty, and Kay Mussell has described a similar character in gothic romances in her article, "Beautiful and Damned: The Sexual Woman in Gothic Fiction."[24] In all of these cases, the function of the rival woman in the novel is to act as a foil to the heroine, who is the central character.

The final person in the Harlequin cast of characters is the rival man. Although he is sketchily outlined, he is contrasted to the hero and rejected by the heroine. We must look at why he is rejected to understand the masculine ideal of Harlequin Romances.

Rival men are either attractive without being handsome or they are "preposterously good looking," as one author put it. Their handsomeness, unlike the heroes', is based on smooth regular features – a little too smooth, a little too regular. They are usually slender in comparison to the massive bulk of the heroes, even verging on the effeminate, with carefully trimmed curls and elegant wrists. Invariably one of their physical features reflects their inner nature: their chin may betray a lack of strength or their lower lip a trace of petulance. Overall, they are suavely, boyishly attractive with carefully cultivated rakishness and style, although there is a minority of tall, sturdily built rugged rivals.

Correspondingly, rival men can be divided into roughly two personality types. The majority are charming, flattering playboys who are fun to go out with but are not considered to be "good husband material" because they are egotistical, superficial, manipulative, unscrupulous, basically weak and, sometimes, physically violent. The minority of rival men are serious, conscientious, a little pompous, dependable and honourable. This type of man is dear but deadly dull and equally to be avoided as a husband, although he is more tempting than the playboy. Heroines may be temporarily engaged to the solid rivals.

Rival men are usually older than the heroines but younger than the heroes. There is even a teenage rival in one older Harlequin although he is obviously unsuitable:

> Peter looked so young in his tight trousers. He hadn't really filled out yet into manhood, she noticed with surprise.[25]

(Is this description intentionally raunchy or merely ingenuous?) This pattern is repeated for every social characteristic. Rival men are more powerful, better educated, more wealthy than heroines, but almost always less so than heroes.

The rival man has the least well-defined literary history of the Harlequin characters although many romances present unsatisfactory male figures who compete for the heroine's love. Joanna Russ describes a similar male figure in gothic novels, the "Shadow-Male," who appears to be protective, responsible and calm but who turns out to be an insane murderer intent on killing the heroine.[26] This character plays a more central role in the gothic than the Harlequin rival man. In addition, his weaknesses are more extreme, although the Harlequin rival is evolving in the direction of the Shadow-Male. In recent romances, the rival man is becoming increasingly violent towards the heroine.

The social importance of the rival man lies in his contrast to the hero, the ideal man whose sterling qualities are highlighted by the rival man's weaknesses and faults. While the hero lives up to David and Brannon's descriptions of the proscribed male sex role – No Sissy Stuff, The Big Wheel, The Sturdy Oak and Give 'Em Hell – the rival man fails.

The rival man completes the Harlequin cast of characters, each of whom has literary and social significance, but the crux of the romances is the way in which these characters relate and interact. The next two chapters will examine their relationships, compare the portrayals of men, women and relationships to reality, and begin to explain the appeal of Harlequin romances.

*

CHAPTER FIVE

ROMANTICIZED REALITY

"It's all right, my little one," he crooned, stroking her hair. "You're safe now, and with me you always will be safe!"

Pathway of Roses
Mary Whistler

If wishes were horses, beggars would ride.

Romances are changing in generally positive ways, yet negative images of women persist. Women are still portrayed to be marginal workers with little commitment to the labour force, who work for "pin money" rather than for necessities. Heroines are still helpless, politically unconscious individuals who want to be dominated by heroes. Moreover, not all the innovations in recent Harlequins are positive. Glamourized images of violent sexuality, which were seldom found in romances published ten years ago or more, are now common. Harlequins' positive messages are counteracted by the retention and adoption of these inaccurate or destructive images of women and their relationships. This chapter will examine the negative elements in Harlequins' portrayals of women's work in the labour force, their work and role in the home, and their attitudes about love, marriage and sex.

* * *

One of the most significant social changes in North America in the twentieth century has been the influx of women into the paid labour force. Although women, particularly poor and minority women, have always worked outside the home, the cultural ideal that married women should stay in the home as full-time wives and mothers while their husbands provide the income for the family was lived out by the majority of families until the middle of the twentieth century.[1] Women's labour force participation rates soared during the First and Second World Wars as women moved into positions vacated by men, but as soon as the wars ended, women returned to the home, sometimes voluntarily, but frequently involuntarily.

In the 1960s, women began to enter the labour force once more. Changing family patterns, rising costs of living and new job structures led to sizeable increases in women's labour force participation rates, which have been growing steadily ever since. According to both the Canadian and the American 1980 censuses, the majority of women are now in the labour force. The highest participation rates still belong to unmarried women, but the largest single increase has occurred among married women with children under six. Approximately 50 percent in Canada and 60 percent in the United States of this traditionally homebound group have paid jobs outside the home.[2] Despite these remarkable changes, however, traditional images of women and their participation in the labour force are still common in Harlequin romances.

In an earlier chapter, I noted that heroines are being portrayed in a broader range of occupations than before and this is true, particularly in Harlequin's new series. Nevertheless, heroines are still concentrated in occupations that are acceptably feminine – clerical, service and artistic work. In reality, most women do work in the clerical and service areas but not in the artistic area, the most attractive option of the three. According to the Canadian and the American censuses, respectively:

> Traditionally, Canadian women have been employed in very few occupational areas. Data for 1980 do not reveal any substantial changes from previous years. Women are still concentrated in the clerical, sales and service sectors of the economy. In 1980, 62.7% of all female workers were in these occupations ...[3]

> Women continue to be concentrated in clerical and service work. More than one-third of employed women are clerical and kindred workers, with an additional 19 percent who are service workers.[4]

It is no small condemnation of society that Harlequin romances, as limited as they are, portray women in a more diverse range of occupations than they are allowed in reality.

"Women's work" in our society is characterized by low pay. For every dollar a man makes, a woman makes only sixty-two cents: "Women's earnings remain low. And increasingly, women supporting children by themselves are likely to live in poverty."[5] In addition, women in these low-paid positions have little prestige and little control over their work. Most of these facts are ignored in Harlequins; if they are mentioned, they are glossed over or, worse, romanticized. Let us begin with a look at Harlequins' traditional picture of women as employees who are unconcerned about money.

Although exact figures are never given, the large income differences between Harlequin men and women are obvious. Heroes uniformly make more money and own more property than heroines but the latter do not complain by any means. Instead they refer to their "well-paid hours in the office" and vow to generous employers: "'I'll try to earn my renumeration.'"[6] In fact, Harlequin heroines are apparently so well paid that they are willing to take on extra work with no increase in salary and may even reject the employer's offer of additional money. Thus, one heroine who is being promoted from secretary to general manager of a hotel (an unlikely chain of promotion) tells her employer: "'I wouldn't want much salary. I'd be learning myself most of the time....'"[7]

Heroines are either highmindedly unconcerned about something as crass and unromantic as money or they are frightened by it, baffled by business. This stereotype has persisted in romances published recently:

> She frowned, her brow knitting in thought. He knew that she would hand all business matters to him or her lawyer, and leave them to sort it out. She herself didn't like handling money because it frightened her, whatever it was. She preferred other people to do it, to take care of her.[8]

> He went on to talk about money and contracts, and Laura, feeling more uncomfortable by the second, did not really listen. She was glad to let Josh organise the business side of her work, she would not have a clue how to go about it herself.[9]

The belief that women shouldn't have to concern their "pretty little heads" over money, that it is unfeminine to negotiate for salaries and so on, has hindered women in their attempts to achieve financial equality with men, and these beliefs linger on in Harlequins.

Heroines do equally little to change or protest other negative aspects of women's work and sometimes even adapt themselves to humiliating working conditions. In one Harlequin, the heroine-secretary is quite aware that her employer has no interest in her or consideration for her as a person. Instead he regards secretaries as "'useful appendages for holding pencils ..., to take down letters and attend to other clerical duties of the firm.'" Nevertheless she is not resentful or indignant:

> "I took my work very seriously.... I intended to be successful, so I adopted the sort of attitude I thought you would want. If you wanted just another piece of office furniture about you, you could have it."[10]

In another novel, the heroine-secretary is required by the hero, her employer, who is an author and works at home, not only to do the usual secretarial tasks but to "tidy up." The rival man, the hero's brother and heroine's current boyfriend, is incensed at this: "'You'd no right to turn Isobel into a char,' Nigel told his brother shortly. 'She's a trained secretary and that's what you're paying her for.'" Remember, the rival man is the negative role model so not surprisingly, the heroine defends the hero and his right to use her as he wishes. She insists that she does not mind tidying up, that she likes being kept busy and points out "'that there's more to being a secretary than shorthand and typing.'"[11]

Heroines are more feisty now, so they are more likely to tell the hero to make his own damned coffee if they are confronted with masculine condescension, but just as that problem begins to disappear, another takes its place that is more insidious. Increasingly, when heroines are working for heroes, as is frequently the case, they are subjected to sexual harassment. Of course, it is not interpreted as such within the stories because the heroine is in love with the hero and ultimately marries him, but it *is* sexual harassment – which has been defined as "any unwanted sexually based or sexually oriented practice which creates discomfort and/or threatens a woman's personal well-being or functioning (mental, physical or emotional)."[12] Sexual harassment permeates the workplace in Harlequin Romances: indeed, it is an essential, titillating part of the plot. The element of unwillingness or coercion adds to the excitement and tension of the romance, as one can see in the following two examples.

The first example of the continued acceptance of intolerable working conditions and sexual harassment occurs in Nicola West's *Lucifer's Brand,* published in April 1983, in which the heroine is a hotel assistant working for the hero, who owns and operates a chain of hotels. He informs her that they will be leaving on a business trip for several days the next morning. She is taken aback by such short notice and protests that she may have had other plans, but her objections are forcefully dismissed:

"... if I say I want to take a trip somewhere and need you along, then I expect you to be free to come, get it? So when you start this hectic social whirl you're obviously expecting to get going, you just remember that and plan accordingly, O.K.?"

"I see!" Flair exclaimed. "You pay me a salary and that means you've bought me body and soul. I do apologise – I didn't notice that clause in my contract."

The startling blue of his eyes darkened at that, and he took a step towards her. Flair, alarmed, moved quickly but he moved faster. His hand caught her wrist and held it painfully and he drew her closer...."[13]

He kisses her into submission and she is dutifully ready for an early start in the morning. When they get to the island where he is inspecting a future hotel site, the heroine discovers that the island is deserted so they are quite isolated. The new unfurnished hotel has only one double bed, which the hero, her employer, expects her to share. He also expects her to work a twelve-hour day and to do the cooking and cleaning up afterwards. In true Harlequin tradition, she does as she is told, although she draws the line at sharing the bed:

It was on the tip of Flair's tongue to refuse, saying that she was his personal assistant, not chief cook and bottlewasher, but she bit the words back, knowing that they would be unreasonable. While she was preparing the meal, Luke could be continuing with his work; it would be foolish to insist that he took his turn with the chores, thus delaying their return to the mainland.[14]

So much for her spirited rebuke of his arrogant assumption of the day before that she should be at his beck and call; Flair has decided to be "reasonable."

She sleeps in a chair the first night but by the end of the second day, she collapses with exhaustion so he undresses her and puts her to bed, which he shares, in spite of her earlier objections. When they awake in the morning, they begin to make love but then she changes her mind and resists:

"Damn you!" he ground out.... "Do you know what they call women like you?" he demanded savagely as she retreated. "Do you know? And do you know what happens when you try it too often? Just once too often ... that's all it takes. But it's the man who gets the blame, poor bastard."[15]

How quickly and easily sexual harassment is turned into the traditional accusation that women get raped because they ask for it!

After these incidents, Flair decides to quit but her father has a big contract with the hero and she is afraid to jeopardize his job. She continues to work for the hero, continues to deal with the explosive sexual tension, continues to be exposed to his advances and his verbal abuse of her – until they both admit that they really love each other. This abrupt turnabout, which the reader can anticipate because she knows that romances have a "happy ending," denies the seriousness of the sexual harassment that preceded the declaration of love. It was all just a silly lovers' game that is simply resolved by a little communication.

The other example is from a story by Sally Wentworth, who frequently confronts issues of sexism in her books. Her heroines are unusual characters who are not afraid to call heroes chauvinist pigs if the situation warrants it (which is usually the case). Wentworth tackles the issue of sexual harassment more directly than other romance writers but even she is constrained by the traditional romance formula and sex-role dynamics. In *Flying High,* the heroine, Leigh, a commerical pilot, has signed a contract with the hero, who does not approve of women pilots and who has managed to slip a clause into her contract giving him the right to fire her if she upsets anyone on his staff, including himself. When he makes a pass at her, she responds but then resists when she realizes that he merely wants to have an affair, a realization that sparks memories of her contract:

> "Just what kind of a man are you?" she demanded furiously. "You treat me like dirt, tell me that you're going to get rid of me just as soon as you can, then expect me to fall into your bed the first time you make a pass!" A thought occurred to her that made her gasp. "Or is going to bed with you a condition of keeping my job? Is that it? If I let you make love to me you'll let me stay on at Allerton's?"
>
> For a moment he stood silently, just staring at her, then he said slowly, "What would your answer be if I said it was?"
>
> "I'd say keep your job," Leigh retorted at once. "And you can just go to hell, Bryce Allerton! I was right about you the first time I met you. I thought then that you were nothing but a womaniser. Only I didn't know just how low you'd stoop to ..."
>
> She broke off abruptly as Bryce grabbed her other arm and shook her angrily. "Have you finished?"

"No, I haven't. I think you're nothing but a ..."

His hand came up suddenly and gripped her throat, so that she stopped abruptly. "I've had about as much as I'm going to take from you, young lady. So just shut up, will you?"[16]

The possibility of sexual harassment is dealt with more openly in this passage than in other romances but even here, it is transformed from an injustice done to her to an injustice done to him. He is stunned by her accusation and then, ever so subtly and adroitly, he turns the incident into a test of *her* character, not his. Will she refuse and be worthy of marriage to him or is she weakly promiscuous? Sexual harassment is reduced from an illegal act that traumatizes its victims to a meaningful compatibility test for potential marriage partners. Leigh passes the test and the hero succeeds in diverting her because that is the last direct charge of sexual harassment we hear from her.

Flying High is particularly interesting because Wentworth incorporates not just one case of sexual harassment in the workplace, but two – an "acceptable" case between the hero and the heroine (already described) and an unacceptable case between the heroine and a client of the flying service. The client seems polite and thoughtful until he tries to rape Leigh in the plane flying at an altitude of 6500 feet in an effort to join the "Mile High Club." She is terrified but manages to fight him off and land the plane. The hero is enraged when he learns about the incident and beats the client up to avenge her, conveniently forgetting that he has sexually threatened her as well.

What is the difference between these two incidents that makes one seduction and one sexual harassment? Very little, and that is the problem. On the surface, the incidents are similar – the heroine faces unwanted, even violent, sexual advances from men she encounters in the context of her work. If anything, the violation should be less threatening from a client than an employer because the employer has more power over her, but the situation is portrayed in reverse. The only difference, and in Harlequins this is the crucial difference, is that the heroine eventually loves the hero-employer. Wentworth bases her distinction between acceptable and unacceptable sexual harassment on the motivations of the men involved. The hero is motivated by repressed love while the client is motivated by disreputable emotions, a desire to boast about his sexual adventures.

Regardless of motivation, however, the action is the same and the consequences experienced by the woman who is being harassed are the same. The hero's ultimately "good intentions" towards the heroine should not be used to justify his sexual harassment. Harlequins obscure the issue of violence against women by romanticizing sexual harassment.

The acceptance of sexual harassment by heroines is all the more serious because the new heroines are portrayed as strong, smart women. Obviously their feistiness does not save them from repeating the same mistakes and falling victim to the same delusions as their wimpish predecessors. They too succumb in the space of 180 pages. The fact that the heroines end up marrying the boss does not change the seriousness of the sexual harassment that preceded the marriage. In fact, the possibility of marrying the boss is yet another form of the glamourization of women's work. This outcome, which is a commonplace event in Harlequins, is rare in real life and it obscures the need for changing women's work. Harlequins try to teach us that it doesn't matter if women make low wages because after all, they are going to marry the prosperous boss and quit their jobs anyway. This brings us to another aspect of the portrayal of women and work in Harlequins – their job commitment.

Harlequins applaud women's work in the labour force as long as it does not affect their femininity and as long as the women do not become career women. Work is seen as necessary for a full and useful life (while single) and Harlequin heroines are generally enthusiastic about their work until they meet the heroes. After this, heroines are no longer able to concentrate and begin to have doubts about their ambition and their commitment to their work. Although they may have struggled to establish a career earlier, suddenly their efforts seem meaningless, their work empty:

> She would, she thought, probably marry him quite soon and settle down, for all of a sudden she saw the prospect of life as a secretary far less attractive.[17]

Given the status and pay of secretarial work, one can appreciate this realization but the same doubt strikes heroines in nontraditional, professional or artistic occupations:

> a horse jumper:
> "I love you, Nick. I always will."
> "Enough to give up jumping for?" he insisted.

"If you want me to." Her reply was without any pause. "It isn't important now."[18]

a hotel manager assistant:

"How do you feel, Flair, about being a wife and mother? Or does your career mean more to you ...?"

Flair thought for a moment. Then she said: "No. Not any more. There was a time when I thought it did – when I thought my career was more important than marriage could ever be. But that was before I met you."[19]

Consistently over the years, work is transformed into an unsatisfactory, unfulfilling chore compared to the satisfying prospect of marriage and motherhood. Being a career woman means more than simply having a long-term commitment to an occupation. Harlequins assume that a career woman has a specific type of personality that precludes her from having a loving relationship. The blissful image of being a loving wife and mother is continually compared to the daunting image of being a career woman who is usually characterized as cold, hard and either promiscuous or sexless, the opposite of what our society believes women should be. Career commitment is all right for a man, but not for a woman:

"You're not a woman – you're a machine. All you can think about is your modelling."

"And what about you" she'd flung back. "Isn't your job important? You talk about it enough."

"It's different for a man. This is my life, my career."[20]

Even women in feminine occupations like modelling do not escape censure if they are committed to their work in a way that is not "feminine." But most heroines are not so ambitious. If circumstances force them to be career women (a bad love affair that turned them sour on life and people so they turn to work as a solace and escape; a dependent child they must support), they are uncomfortable in the role; and when the heroes accuse them of being unnatural, inhuman Amazons, they know these charges are correct. The heroine in *Between Pride and Passion* by Flora Kidd, for example, is painfully aware of the contrast between the real Karen Carne, who is a "sensitive, wide-eyed, freely-loving girl," and the new Karen Carne, who is a "poised career woman fully in control of her own life and her child's." It has taken her seven long years to achieve this pose, but after she meets the hero and falls in love with him, her composure slips and even the insensitive rival man realizes that he has not known the real Karen: "'Oh, you've done a good job of pretending, covering up with that disguise you're so good at hiding behind, the mask of the cool, collected career woman.'"[21] Karen is soon transformed by the hero back to her natural self:

> In a few moments Karen had changed from the cool, level-headed, almost sexless person she had prided herself in being for the past few years into a purely sensual woman, glorying in her knowledge of her mature and softly rounded body, luxuriating in the way it was coming alive under the tender touch of Val's fingers.[22]

Being a career woman is a "stage" some women go through because they haven't met the right man; it is a state of limbo. Neither alive nor dead, heroines wait for their princes to awaken them with a kiss and save them from a life without love.

These allusions to career women are benign compared to some. In *Liberated Lady*, the hero tells the career woman-heroine what he thinks of her and women like her:

> "You career women are all the same – you're so busy beating men down in your fight to get to the top that you lose all your femininity. And you're so insecure and afraid of losing what you've gained that you brow-beat others into doing what you want."[23]

She denies it, of course, but "deep down" she has serious doubts about her ability to love and to maintain intimate relationships. Success in work notwithstanding, she feels like a complete failure and she acknowledges that the hero comes painfully close in another contemptuous attack:

> "What a coward you are, Sara!" Afraid to commit yourself to marriage and even more afraid to share even a part of yourself.... You've told yourself so often that you don't need a man that you're too full of inhibitions even to go to bed with one. Why Sara? Because you're too terrified of losing one iota of your precious freedom? Or it is because you know deep down that that's really what you want? To give yourself utterly to a man and let him have complete mastery of you."[24]

For the heroine to win the hero and happiness, she must learn to distance herself from her work and give herself to him. Of course, she does and the book ends: "He laughed softly, his mouth against her neck, and said happily, 'You know, Sara, I'm going to make a female chauvinist of you yet!'"

Most heroines in earlier romances gave up their full-time work after marriage. Recent romances tend to avoid portraying this outcome as inevitable although it is desirable. Some Harlequins evade the issue altogether by not indicating whether the heroine will continue to work after marriage. Most romances "compromise": if, at the end of the novel, a heroine plans to work, it is either to do part-time freelance work in the home or to assist her husband in his work.

Heroines' shaky commitment to the labour force is consistent with the view that women's work is unnecessary and unimportant both in terms of the economy and their lives. This perspective of women as a marginal labour force, which Pat Connelly has called the "consumer choice approach," maintains that "married women make a conscious choice whether or not to enter the labour force and this choice is determined by subjective factors over which they have some control."[25] Harlequins depict women's labour force participation as a continual moving in and out of the work force. The decision to remain in or to leave the labour force is a choice that women are free to make according to their own and their husbands' personal preferences and values. This view of women's labour force participation focuses on subjective factors like women's "desire to work," not the objective factor of financial need, which is that most women are economically obliged to work to support themselves or their families.

The image of women and work in Harlequins reinforces some of the notions that have been used to justify isolating women into low-status positions that allow no job autonomy and pay poorly. These notions include the belief that women are not committed to their work and have high rates of turnover; that married women are free to choose whether they want to work or not according to their personal preferences; that married women work for social reasons or for "pin money" and not because they need a livable wage; and that women are a sexy distraction in the labour force. Employers can and have justified the use of women as a cheap labour force by citing these beliefs, which Harlequins continue to accept and perpetuate.

* * *

Stereotypical images of women's role in the home also persist in society and in Harlequins. Traditionally, work in the home has been seen as women's true work and vocation. Women are believed to have a special, natural talent for domestic labour while men are supposedly inept and uncomfortable in the home environment. Harlequins portrayed and reinforced this sexual division of labour within the home for many years. As late as 1976, one could find heroes uttering such classic lines as "I always believe in leaving the homemaking bits to the little woman" and heroines were happy to be doing them.[26] Women were capable of miraculously transforming a house into a home, and heroines jealously guarded this prerogative, feeling threatened when the heroes proved to be self-sufficient:

> She would jolly well stay to lunch and see just how well he could manage without a woman to do it for him. The disappointing thing was that when they sat down to the meal she had to admit that he seemed to manage extremely well.[27]

> What a breakfast! ... really, no one would have believed this came from a bachelor household. Well, she'd heard that most New Zealand men could cook a snack when needed but this was so good it made her feel superfluous.[28]

Harlequins have moved away from simplistic portrayals of a strict domestic sexual division of labour but they still glamourize women's work in the home and gloss over the drawbacks, just as they do for women's work in the labour force. First of all, after they are married, heroines have almost unlimited money to spend. Although they are not paid directly for their labour – that would be regarded as an insult and a sign of a lack of affection – their husbands are generous, providing more than ample household money and personal presents like jewelry, clothes and furs. In contrast, Ann Oakley, in her early 1970s study of housewives, found that one of the reasons women disliked their work in the home was that they were usually operating under severe financial constraints.[29] They could not afford conveniences that would save them time and energy; they had to strictly budget and shop for "bargains," which frequently turned out to be inferior goods that they not only disliked but that quickly wore out and had to be replaced at more expense and effort. These strains are not faced by Harlequin heroines. They may have to scrimp when they are single but not once they marry, because heroes are wealthy men.

Secondly, the future wealth of the heroines means that many of them will have paid help for work in the home, which is infrequently the case in reality. This portrayal glosses over the social isolation and the amount of work that most housewives face alone in the home. Thirdly, because married heroines have paid help, they can choose which of the household tasks they will do and which they will leave for their help. This arrangement allows Harlequins to portray women doing pleasurable, creative household tasks like occasional cooking, entertaining, gardening and decorating, and avoid the depiction of women doing unpleasant, repetitive and boring tasks like cleaning, washing and ironing. It also gives heroines the freedom and flexibility they wanted when they left the labour force.

Earlier Harlequins focused more on domesticity than current ones, which have switched their main appeal to sexuality, but neither the old nor the new Harlequins pay specific attention to women's actual work in the home. Instead they emphasize consumption, a more enjoyable preoccupation than the production and maintenance of everyday necessities. Thus, they are able simultaneously to draw on women's interests in personal and household goods and to avoid reminding women of their tedious role in connection with these goods. Harlequins' portrayal of food preparation is a good example.

Heroines are never faced with the three-times-a-day inevitability of meal preparation, serving and cleaning up. Instead, most of the food they eat is prepared by invisible others in elegant restaurants or by housekeepers in private homes. Sometimes the food is described in "luscious" detail:

> But the dinner was heavenly.... the steak and mushrooms were perfectly grilled, the baked jacket potatoes artistically cupped in slit foil, the vegetables obviously home-grown and flavoury. The pavlova was all a pavlova should be, crisply sugary on the outside, marshmallow-soft inside, filled with a delectable mixture of fruit and cream and tangy with the passion-fruit pulp ...[30]

The abundant use of descriptive adjectives glamourizes the meal. Focusing exclusively on the consumption of the product obscures the fact that most meals are the product of labour, usually women's unpaid labour in the home.

The focus on food and cooking in the novels extended into the monthly magazine that Harlequin published at one time. Along with a full-length novel, short stories and travel articles, it featured a cooking section with recipes from around the world, some drawn directly from the romances. Harlequin no longer publishes the magazine but occasionally there is a recipe at the back of a Harlequin Presents. For example:

A Traditional Italian Dish

> When Laura dines on Spaghetti Bolognese she is treating herself to a delicious and nourishing traditional pasta dish enjoyed by lovers of

Italian food everywhere. Here's a simple recipe that will feed the whole family![31]

Readers respond to the novels' and magazine's interest in food by writing to the company to thank them for recipes and to request others:

> Many of the recipes have become standard favorites of our family; not only that, I find that I read the description of food in the stories more carefully and wonder if they will soon be included in the magazine.[32]

> I hope you never stop printing the recipes taken from the romances. It's such a pleasure to cook them and feel that even if you know it's make-believe, someone in that country might really be cooking the same for her family. I always go find the book and end up reading it all over again.[33]

An interesting double effect is that Harlequins not only glamourize food preparation and consumption but also reinforce the reading of Harlequins.

Harlequins also emphasize personal consumer goods like clothes, makeup and jewelry. Women are traditionally believed to be preoccupied with their appearance; presenting themselves in the best possible light is considered not only an area of expertise and enjoyment, but a duty. Harlequins are consistent with this sex-role stereotype and the books supply women readers with extensive descriptions of characters' personal appearances. The older books prudishly stress cleanliness:

> She was dressed very simply in a pleated navy skirt and a blue and white striped shirt, with a broad black patent belt cinching her waist. Her hair, teeth, and nails shone with cleanliness. One knew at a glance that her underwear would be as fresh and immaculate as her outer clothes...[34]

while the newer books stress sexiness:

> ... Lesley went up to her room and changed into a short, cool wrap-around skirt which emphasised the slenderness of her waist while its dead-whiteness enhanced the soft tan the afternoons beside the pool have given her legs. With it she teamed a tight red cotton-knit top, simple but sexy since it was sleeveless and plunged sharply in front.[35]

Almost every Harlequin pays close attention to dress, hair, accessories and makeup in passages that both glamourize and instruct. One may learn that "one doesn't smother oneself in French perfume. A discreet drop is all that's necessary"; that one wears certain colours to show off one's tan; that one wears the right style to accent one's slenderness or curvaceousness; and that the appropriate jewels can dramatically change a simple gown into a lovely creation. Knowing how to apply makeup, to style hair and choose clothes is regarded as an art and is a quality in a woman, even a rival woman, that is always admired in Harlequins.

Harlequins' emphasis on feminine attractiveness is, unfortunately, a fairly realistic assessment of the importance of beauty for women in our society. Most women who want to have a heterosexual love relationship are forced to be concerned about their appearance and its impact on men. A number of studies have shown that a woman's physical attractiveness has a notable impact on whether a man will consider her to be a dating or marriage partner, whether he will help her when she needs assistance and how aggressively he will treat her.[36] A woman's appearance also affects her education and occupation, important determinants of socioeconomic well-being in our society.[37]

The message in Harlequins is that there is no need or excuse for a woman to be unattractive because a little makeup and hairstyling can transform a plain woman into a beauty. Some Harlequins, for example, *Rising Star* published in 1969 and *The Judas Kiss,* published in 1982, describe the artificial transformation of "an ugly duckling" into a swan, similar to features in women's magazines that have a before and after picture of women who are "made over." The underside of the promise that any woman can be attractive is the rebuke that she has only herself to blame if she does not try to improve her appearance. Attaining and maintaining beauty is a form of achievement in our society that is reinforced by Harlequins.

* * *

Harlequins have added a third element to the song that begins: "Love and marriage, love and marriage, go together like a horse and carriage ..." – and that element is sex. Apart from this addition, however, the sentiments expressed in that old song remain largely unchanged in contemporary Harlequins. The triumvirate of love, sex and marriage comprises not only the essence of the romances but of life itself, according to prevailing Harlequin philosophy. All other interests and activities fade in significance: "... it really is love that makes the world go around. Without it you are nothing, absolutely nothing."[38] The recently injected realism in Harlequins does not challenge this article of faith. To the contrary, the awareness of social problems and injustice reinforces the idea that people desperately need love to counterbalance these destructive forces. The message in Harlequins is that as the public world becomes increasingly inhospitable, personal life remains the sole refuge for the troubled. When the heroine in Alexandra Sellers' *Season of Storm* learns about the racism and facism (a term used in the novel) endemic in Canadian society, she feels the world shake under her feet: "'Nothing's safe, is it?' she whispered." But the hero replies: "'I used to think that nothing was safe.... But that isn't true. Love is safe ...'"[39] Although in other contexts, Harlequins hint that love is not so safe either, generally the romances encourage the retreat into personal life.

Since love is the all-important thing in a person's life, no pallid, tepid love will do. Love must be intense, consuming and uncontrollable. There can be little mistake about what Harlequins regard as love because they meticulously describe the symptoms – hearts race, pulses pound, bodies tremble and knees go weak. These extreme physical sensations are triggered by minimal bodily contact with or even the mere sight of the love object. For example, in the following quotation, the hero and heroine are simply dancing:

> Lesley could feel her bones beginning to melt, she slipped into a kind of mental swoon, aware only of the man who held her in his arms.... Close to him like this, her body was criss-crossed with the craziest feelings – the sharp pains of delight and desire went through her like knives, taking her breath and leaving her spent, almost gasping, weak as water. She felt herself slacken, and then in reaction tense nervously ...[40]

The intensity is all the more exaggerated by the fact that the person experiencing these crazy feelings has no control over them. The hero or heroine is driven by heterosexual instinct, which they unsuccessfully try to suppress:

> Secretly astounded by her own behaviour, Lisa found she could not help it. For once natural instinct was having its way with her, pushing aside the dictates of her will no matter how hard she tried to assert that strong and highly-developed faculty.[41]

Love is irrational and cannot be controlled by reason or will; the heart has a mind of its own. Even when a hero thinks "the worst" of a heroine, he cannot stop loving her. Even when a hero is seemingly cruel and unobtainable, the heroine cannot stop loving him:

"How can you love a man like that?"

"I don't know, Jonathan," she said drearily. "Love's never been known for its logic, has it? It would probably be much better for me if I could fall in love with you – you're kind and considerate, I know you'd be good to me. But I can't, Jonathan. I'm sorry – I just can't."[42]

This resignation is yet another example of the powerlessness and acquiescence to "fate" typical of Harlequins. Events and emotions happen to people but people seldom make their own destinies. While it is true that emotions are not always logical and there is much in life out of one's control, people do have some control over what they feel and how they act upon their emotions. Certainly the evidence about marriage patterns indicates that people do not fall blindly in love with individuals who would be judged inappropriate by their reference groups. Most people marry partners who are roughly the same age, who come from the same social class, religion, race or ethnic group, who have the same educational level and even who are physically similar to themselves. One scholar concludes: "Cupid's arrow, then does not strike at random."[43] Socially patterned marriages in a society where marriage is supposed to be based on love is a strong indication that people learn to fall in love with "the right people" and that individuals can control emotions – even love, although "love has never been known for its logic."

The romanticization of reality is also evident in Harlequins' portrayals of the balance of power within marriage. As we shall see in the next chapter, many heroines maintain they want equal love relationships but their quest for equality is seriously undermined by the contradictory values they espouse and their socioeconomic background. In a study of the effect external factors have on the distribution of power in marriage, Dair Gillespie found that the following variables were the most important: age, wealth, occupation, education, social contacts and physical size.[44] Power in these areas carries over into marriage. Heroes have the edge on heroines for all of these factors; they are older, more educated, wealthier, bigger and more influential. The heroes' elevated social positions are flaunted throughout the books and occasionally a hero's status is such an essential part of how he sees himself and of how the heroine sees him that it cannot be ignored even in their most intimate moments:

Down in the speed boat the oil boss swung Sarah aboard.... She would have to start calling him Bryce. Soon now he would be her husband.

The engine roared. As they thundered away Sarah let her gaze rest on his dark shape with a loving tender light.

Dear as he was to her heart, she would always think of him as *the oil boss.*[45]

"You didn't need me any more?"

"Not as ombudsman ... But" ... a long deliberate pause ... "how does Mrs. Corporation Boss sound?"

"Mrs. – But you're the Corporation Boss."

"I believe it's what I'm called."

"Then Mrs. Corporation Boss would mean – "

"Yes, it would mean the wife of the boss, Miss Searle."[46]

These examples indicate very clearly the balance of power between a typical hero and heroine. He *is* the boss!

This imbalance does not greatly trouble the new heroines because they still cherish traditional values in spite of their accomplishments and spirit:

At heart she was an old-fashioned girl who needed an old-fashioned man, the kind who instinctively protected and cherished all women, and particularly one who belonged to him. She didn't want to be equal: she wanted to be complementary.[47]

Complementary – as in you're so strong and I'm so weak, as in you're so rational and I'm so emotional, as in you're so rich and I'm so poor, as in you're so powerful and I'm so powerless.

Once heroines fall in love, instead of fighting male mastery, they are thrilled by it. Heroines particularly want the heroes to dominate their sexual relationships. It is either understood or stated explicitly that heroes are sexually experienced and good lovers. They are so attractive and "supremely male," so "potently masculine," so "obviously virile" that it would be impossible for them to be as inexperienced as the heroines for, after all, a man has "needs." Women, on the other hand, do not have "needs" or, if they do, they must suppress them until after love and marriage because heroes still prefer inexperienced women: "'I was looking for somebody like you, a girl who wanted me for her first lover.'"[48] Although Harlequins frequently include premarital sex, heroines and heroes believe that a woman shouldn't go to bed with a man until they are married. The typical heroine stoutly maintains that she will not have an affair even if it costs her the relationship and the hero respects her for that although he can usually convince her to change her mind by the end of the book. This "slip," however, is justified because they are in love. The reader knows this even if the lovers do not at the time.

Whether they wait until marriage or not, the hero is the dominant sexual partner. Judith Long Laws and Pepper Schwartz note that in the traditional sexual script for men and women "the woman is essentially ignorant, the man experienced. If a woman is without substantial sexual experience, sexual initiation is a specific kind of learning experience. The male is cast as the teacher."[49] This describes the basic image of female sexuality in Harlequins. Until the sexual awakening, which takes place within the bonds of marriage or at least a love relationship, the heroine suppresses her sexuality and remains essentially pure, even prudish, blushing at the mention of kisses, babies and beds. If the hero and heroine go to bed before they confess their love for each other, the heroine is deeply ashamed of her sexual response:

> He went out and closed the door and she fumbled herself into the nightie and lay down, pulling the covers over her again. She was sick with self-hatred. She knew that while Lee was holding her, kissing, caressing her, she had been craving far more than what he was actually doing, and she despised herself.[50]

> Shame and humiliation coursed through her like a heated flame, scorching her dignity and her pride. She ought to hate Greg for reducing her to the level of a harlot, but she could not; not when she thought of her own eager participation in what had occurred between them and, squirming inwardly in self-disgust, she leapt out of bed and dressed herself as quickly as her trembling fingers would allow.[51]

The sexual double standard and traditional sex-role socialization have been internalized by these heroines, but their ashamed reaction is nothing compared to the anger the men feel if they believe that the heroines have "compromised" themselves. Quick to believe "the worst," heroes automatically condemn heroines if there is any hint of sexual exploration:

> "It was a bitter blow to find that fellow there when I took you home. I didn't want to believe ... that you were that sort of girl."[52]

This passage is not dated: heroines are called tramps, sluts and tarts more than ever before. If heroes believe heroines are sexually promiscuous they do not draw the line at name calling:

> He picked her up in his arms and carried her to his room, kicking the door shut behind them. She was struggling like a wild thing, biting and

scratching, but he didn't even seem to notice.

As he threw her across the bed, she sobbed out, "Dane – no! Please – no!"

His mocking smile made him look like a devil as he tossed the dressing gown aside and bent over her. "Yes, Lisa, please, yes." His voice altered and roughened. "Sluts don't have a choice, darling. And you've forfeited yours."[53]

Despite the "sexual revolution," women are still punished for expressing their sexuality, whether in Harlequins or in real life. Although the category of virgin has been stretched to include one sexual partner within the bonds of love, women are still seen as either pure or evil, virgins or whores, angels or temptresses. Much of the contemporary romantic plot revolves around the hero's attempt to figure out which sort of girl the heroine is and the book's happy ending arises out of his realization that she is not a slut after all or, better yet, she *is* but only with him. Before love and marriage, heroines must make every attempt to kill their sexuality in order to be socially acceptable, but they are also expected to be able to suddenly revive their sexuality after they fall in love. Once the hero and heroine are paired, any sexual awkwardness or reluctance on her part is not regarded as a sign of virtuous worth but rather as childishness or frigidity. Heroes make it plain that after marriage they will not put up with the maidenly scruples they required initially:

> "Do I appear to you ... the type to put up with *that* sort of marriage?" He demanded it harshly, directly, inclining his head to the single bedroom. "Do you think I'd be the kind to bear with half-measures, Miss Royden? Do you? ... I would *not* be that type, Miss Royden. I would expect and demand entirety, fulfillment, conclusion, a completion to a logical end. Do you understand?"[54]

When unmarried, heroines must avoid being "that sort of girl" but after marriage they must become "that sort of girl" to avoid having "that sort of marriage." In Harlequins, this is accomplished with ease because loving a man is synonymous with being sexually attracted to him. More significantly, being sexually attracted to a man is synonymous with loving him. Men may enjoy love and sex separately but women may not. So heroines reverse course and become sexually responsive because they are in love. Laws and Schwartz demonstrate the essential passivity of this response:

> Romantic love affords the delights of passive abandonment.... Identifying and giving oneself up to love permits the individual woman to

have what she wants, without exercising force (or even volition). In love, she is not responsible.[55]

Because Harlequin heroines do not want to be responsible for their sexuality, they even go to the extreme of wishing the hero would rape them to relieve them of the burden of choice:

She needed the masterful touch – the removal of choice. It was the only way she could let herself go and respond to emotions of which she was basically ashamed.[56]

She wanted him to exert his strength, dominate her with the power of his arms, impose his will with the passion of his mouth.[57]

... part of her almost wished that he would physically impose himself on her and thus relieve her of the burden of making her own decision ...[58]

Caught in the dilemma of wanting the hero but being unable to say so for fear of rejection and contempt, the heroine sends double messages. She says no when she means yes and the hero is left to interpret the result as he wishes: "'Your lips say one thing, but your eyes speak differently,' he chided her mocking. 'I wonder which I should believe?'"[59] He knows, and the reader knows, that the heroine really wants the hero to ignore her protests. This is made apparent on the few occasions when the hero does leave her alone as she demands. Her reaction is depression and disappointment:

The tears fell, tears of anger and helplessness, and disappointment that her husband was a weakling, and not masterful as she now knew she wanted him to be.... She didn't want to be terrified ... no, just made to feel a little apprehensive of her husband ...[60]

The "complementary" sexual and love relationship that heroines crave is rather easily corrupted by unequal power dynamics into family violence. The combination of helplessness, emotional intensity, male dominance and possessiveness is explosive. Heroes and heroines accept violent jealousy as a sign of Real Love. Consequently they try to provoke their loved ones into jealous displays and heroes boast of the extent of their jealousy in their declarations of love: "'I think I'd break your neck if you allowed someone else to give you so much as a chaste salute on the forehead. You're going to find me fiendishly jealous.'"[61] Never mind that breaking her neck or threatening to do so is an excessive (to say the least) reaction to a chaste salute on the forehead; never mind that such extreme possessiveness characterizes wife abusers in our society; never mind that women have been taught to be victims who are held immobile in the grips of what some scholars call learned helplessness – heroines make no protest. On the contrary, they are thrilled by the hero's jealousy and his threats. In these portrayals, love is indistinguishable from hate:

> "I hate you!" she hissed, straining against the arms that held her.
> "Hate is a very positive emotion, and I think I like it. The more you hate me, my dear Caroline, the more I find that I want you."[62]

> He had hated her with a burning intensity only because he had loved her so deeply. His hatred was as strong as his love. And that was what made her mind up for her. When a man loves you as much as that, she reasoned happily, how can you turn him down?[63]

How indeed? It is a perverted, destructive form of logic that interprets violence and hate as an expression of great love but such logic is common in Harlequins.

If love is mixed with hate, it is not surprising that sex should be used as punishment. Angry kisses are more the rule than the exception in Harlequins. Sometimes the heroine is very aware of the hero's motivation:

> Without giving her a chance to speak again, he crushed her roughly closer, and as she lifted her chin to protest, drove his mouth down on hers in a kiss that explained everything without words. It was a punishment in itself ...[64]

Other times the heroine is uncertain: "Go, she pleaded silently. Don't you feel the vibrations in this room? There's anger here but there's something sexual too, and it's making me feel so confused."[65]

Amidst this confusion, the heroine's final realization that the hero's anger, hate and violence is love is a happy relief. Tradition has it that women are mysterious but it is the men who are the enigmas in Harlequins. Confronted with expressionless faces and hooded eyes, heroines are haunted by the fear that they do not know what is going on in the heroes' minds:

> Men were so unpredictable; you could never be sure of their intentions – or their actions.[66]

> Paul on the surface was a cultured Greek, very Westernized in his ways, and in some of his outlooks on life. But what was he beneath that suave urbane veneer of polish? Would she be able to recognise the *real* man if ever he was revealed to her? ... Her mouth was dry; fear was strong within her, fear of the unknown ... yes, of the parts unknown of this man to whom she was married.[67]

Fear, which is an increasingly common plot element in Harlequins, was the main ingredient in the gothic romances that were so popular in the 1960s (Joanna Russ' article on gothics, "Somebody's Trying to Kill Me and I Think It's My Husband" makes this very clear[68]). Harlequin heroines also have reason to fear, since with very few exceptions they will be physically and emotionally hurt by the heroes. For example, the heroines in Penny Jordan's *Blackmail* (1982), Sara Craven's *Dark Summer Dawn* (1982), Kay Thorpe's *The Shifting Sands* (1975) and Margaret Pargeter's *Not Far Enough* (1982) are raped by the heroes. The heroine in *To Tame a Vixen* by Anne Hampson (1979), is spanked by the hero, who comments: "'Silly child to goad me.... I hope the lesson will have the desired result. I'm not at all happy in the role of woman-beater, but on the other hand I don't intend to take any more sauce from you ...'"[69] The heroines in Patricia Lake's *Heartless Love* (1982) and Sally Wentworth's *The Judas Kiss* (1982) are threatened with death and, in the latter book, the hero nearly strangles the heroine:

> He towered over her, the bitter fury plain in his face.... "You bitch! You beautiful, lying bitch!" He gripped her shoulders fiercely, shook her fiercely. "I could kill you for what you did! Do you hear me?" His voice rose furiously and he let go of her shoulders to move his hands up to her throat. "I could wring your lovely neck for what you did to me!"
>
> Lyn moaned, too paralysed by fear to move. She felt his fingers tighten round her throat, begin to squeeze. She looked into the murderous rage in his eyes, and then sickening waves of blackness merged into each other as she collapsed unconscious at his feet.[70]

In gothic romances the man who emerges as the hero has never tried to harm the heroine. Initially there may be some confusion over which male character is the hero. The heroine may think she is in love with and even married to a hero, who instead turns out to be the crazed killer, or she may believe the true hero is the killer when he is not, but in the end, the hero stands revealed as a man who has consistently protected her from harm. In recent Harlequins, however, the very man who has tried to hurt her is the hero. In fact, his ability to frighten her is part of his appeal:

> Women always looked at Alex Brent like that.... His lean, hard body held a menacing sexuality, an implicit threat of sexual violence which attracted women like iron filings to a magnet.[71]

Just as sexual harassment in the labour force is glamourized in Harlequins, these portrayals romanticize sexual violence in "love" relationships. Contemporary Harlequins regularly affirm the notion that women like to be dominated and that violence sexually excites them. As one heroine helplessly admits: "'One doesn't necessarily love the nicest men best.'"[72]

Heroines are not merely the victims of sexual violence; they also perpetuate it. Violent encounters with heroes are frequently escalated by heroines who typically respond to heroes' verbal attacks ("bitch!") with more verbal attacks ("bastard!") and physical force:

> The descent from overwhelming desire to vehement rejection was accomplished in seconds, one arm coming up across his throat with a fierceness that could have snapped his neck had he not been ready for it.[73]

Romance authors probably intend a scene like this to convey the heroine's feistiness, but their good intentions are negated by the harmful messages implicit in these scenes. First of all, portrayals of newly achieved feminine violence overlook the fact that equality of violence is not a particularly desirable goal to pursue. Secondly, the heroine's violence backfires and is used against her by the hero. She appears more foolish than feisty; the message actually conveyed is that it is dangerous to fight back. While resisting a sexual attack may sometimes be unwise in reality, resistance does not inevitably fail, as is typically the case in Harlequins. The heroine's resistance, which initially appears to be a laudable act of self-preservation ultimately reinforces feminine passivity because the heroine is so ineffective in her use of force.

* * *

Romances do not have to reinforce the exploitative beliefs about women and work, sex and marriage described in this chapter. The romance formula could easily be stretched to include more realistic and positive portrayals of women. For example, romances could feature heroines who recognize sexual harassment for what it is rather than accept it as a disguised form of love. Romances could feature heroes who value a woman's job commitment as a sign of her healthy independence, personal integrity and strength of character rather than reject it as a sign of emotional and sexual frigidity. Together the hero and heroine could strive for mutual respect and independence rather than for absorbing love-hate inspired passion. Harlequin Enterprises, its editors and writers, therefore, choose to continue to portray women and men engaging in destructive behaviour and believing in sexist stereotypes that have worked against women in reality.

While romances have retained many harmful images of women, they have also begun to change in some important ways. The next chapter will analyze some of the more positive images of women that are emerging in romances today.

*

CHAPTER SIX

STRANGE BEDFELLOWS:
FEMINISM AND ROMANCE

Knowing him had taught her a lot; that she wasn't willing to sacrifice her career and her independence for marriage and security, and also that she couldn't blithely enter into a cold-blooded sexual relationship. So just what did she want? she wondered wryly. A man who would be warm and loving, but otherwise not make any demands on her time and her freedom, someone who stayed conveniently in the background. She smiled cynically to herself; that sounded more like a wife than a husband!

Liberated Lady
Sally Wentworth

"Aren't you a believer in the liberation of your sex?"
"Of course. What woman wouldn't be?"

For Love of a Pagan
Anne Hampson

Traditional images of women persist in Harlequins, alongside an emerging feminist consciousness that leaves the novels open to many interpretations. Rather like the blind men who each grasp a part of an elephant and therefore come away with a different impression of what an elephant looks like, analysts can read the same Harlequins and find support for very contradictory viewpoints.

Harlequins and Harlequin heroines themselves are openly ambivalent about their values:

Heavens, what a contradiction she was! She wasn't prepared to relinquish an ounce of her freedom, not careerwise or emotionally, and yet she secretly longed to be swept off her feet, to be cherished, to be made to feel the most important thing in some man's life.[1]

This ambivalence will become increasingly clear as we examine the more positive images of women, work, sex and marriage that exist in contrast to the negative images discussed in the last chapter.

* * *

A significant positive element of romance is that they tell the stories of rather ordinary women whose appearance, emotions, thoughts and actions are considered interesting. Since women are frequently relegated to supportive roles in our society, the focus on heroines is an affirmation of women's importance as individuals and actors. More and more often, these ordinary women are strong, spirited women. The new heroine is consistently introduced as a survivor, a fighter or a daredevil (the title of one Harlequin Presents that refers to the heroine, not the hero, as one might assume). Even the traditionally feminine, delicate heroine is an iron butterfly:

> Leonie had more backbone than you might think. She had a hidden core of strength that people didn't suspect as they looked at her slender, fine-boned body and the delicate oval of her small face between those blonde curls.[2]

Heroines have lost some of the treacly niceness that characterized them in the past. Although they are still made up of sugar and spice, the stress is on the spice, as one heroine makes clear in her declaration that: "'I'd hate to be labelled sweet.'"[3] This spirited strength is portrayed to be an inherent part of the heroine's character, an aspect that cannot be taken away from her by adversity, prosperity or even by love. Some authors take care to emphasize this by indicating that the heroine is "independent by nature" or that she has a strong "instinct" for self-preservation. The term "instinct" is used in Harlequins to describe traits that are considered to be an essential part of a person, gender, race or ethnic group. Usually references to "instinct" reinforce racist or sexist stereotypes but in this case, the term is used to convey a positive impression of the enduring quality of the heroine's strength. Used to confidently managing on her own, the new heroine resents the hero's disturbing intrusion into her life:

> She didn't like having her life taken over in this way. It made her feel insecure, unsure of herself.[4]

> It made her feel as if the control of her life was slipping out of her hands, and ... she had grown fiercely independent, valuing that independence above everything else.[5]

The heroine's fear that she will lose her independence to the hero acts as a barrier between them – a relatively new plot device in Harlequins. Earlier heroines had no independence to protect; instead of being threatened by the hero's dominance, they were buoyed up by it. The new heroine is not so eager to surrender her sovereignty to a man.

The new heroine is no longer a retiring, self-sacrificing maiden content to be a daughter until she is a wife. At the beginning of the story, authors quickly establish that heroines are committed to educational achievements and careers. In older Harlequins, heroines were more than willing to set aside their education, occupation and self-interest whenever any family member, friend or even total stranger needed them. Recent heroines are more likely to resemble Laura who, when her family moves a continent away, decides to finish her college education rather than follow them or Jacqueline who, although she believes her sister has a prior first claim on her own fiancé, refuses to obligingly step aside: "... nor had she any intention of playing the self-sacrificing sister and putting her sister's happiness before her own."[6] Still other heroines declare their independence by refusing to accept financial support from their sometimes wealthy families in order to make it on their own.[7] If, by the end of the story, most heroines are more interested in the heroes than in their jobs, they at least enter their marriages knowing that they can take care of themselves. Others who never lose their determination and ambition plan "brilliant careers" for themselves with the full knowledge that they are bright, competent and dedicated.[8]

The emerging feminist consciousness in Harlequins goes beyond incorporating more independent heroines to include pointing out and criticizing sexism in its many forms. This is particularly evident in the romances set in countries that still have very traditional attitudes towards women, like Greece or the Middle East. Heroines are uniformly outraged by the injustice done to women in these societies and they openly denounce "antiquated" customs such as the sexual double standard, dowries, unquestioning obedience of the wife to the husband and sexist property laws. At times like these, they are thankful that they were born in more liberal countries:

> Lorna tried to envisage what her own life would have been like had she been born a Kuwaiti. From cradle to grave she would have been dominated and answerable to father, brother, or husband. It was enough to

make her hackles rise. With all its faults, England was not such a bad place to live after all.[9]

Heroines who remain in their native lands have no invidious comparisons to make to stir gratitude in their hearts for the relative freedom they experience so they chafe against the sexism that they encounter in their own supposedly progressive countries. The general lack of respect for women, their exploitation in the labour force, sexual violence and inequality in marriage all come under attack. Heroines realize that the traditional female sex role has severely limited their lives:

> She had been on the run from reality all her life, it seemed to her. She had been conditioned to see herself in that yielding female role, to accept the qualities that society expected in a woman, to be soft and gentle and pliant, to submit and give what was demanded, she had not been taught to demand in her turn, to be strong and self-sufficient, to claim her right, as a woman, to match the male on her own terms.[10]

A heightened consciousness about inequality means anger and the new heroines are frequently angry women. Although they are annoyed with themselves for complying and for being "yes-girls,"[11] they are even more angry at society and men. First of all, they resent being taken for granted. They believe that men casually assume that they will always be there to provide services, comfort and support. That assumption, however, does not mean that those services are valued by men. One heroine woefully observes a dutiful daughter and thinks: "I cry for us.... All women. Marion left to wilt in the shadow of a domineering father, universally regarded as foolish when she ran a big household and was very good at it. No one took Marion seriously ..."[12]

Secondly, they resent the credibility that men have in the world by virtue of their gender. Heroines are aware that women do not have the same power over others that men do. When a young heroine observes a scene at a party in which the rival woman (Jane) slaps the hero (Mark) after he says something offensive to her, she knows that it is the woman who will suffer from the stigma of the encounter, no matter how justified her reaction:

> She sympathised intensely with Jane; the story of that night's exploits would not affect Mark Taylor at all, it would probably just add to his 'man of the world' image. But the woman would be considered a hysterical fool ...[13]

This example is particularly noteworthy because the heroine is usually pitted against the rival woman but in this passage, the heroine's antagonism is overcome by her anger at sexist injustice.

Thirdly, heroines are angry about being treated as less than human adults. They refuse to be reduced by men to the level of children, dolls, commodities, dumb blondes, objects or property. Frequently the offenders are members of the heroine's family (usually the father) or rival men who must be rejected if the heroine is to achieve her independence. This is a painful process but the heroine knows she has no choice:

> They never wondered how she felt or what she thought – she was like a pretty doll they both treasured and liked to have around, but she wasn't a person to them. She didn't matter, really matter.[14]

Finally, heroines are angry because they are dependent upon men for social approval and protection. In Harlequins, heroines are not only threatened by sexual violence from the heroes but from other men as well. Frequently, in order to save themselves from the latter, they must turn to the former for protection. They are grateful for the hero's protection but they also hate feeling helpless and indebted. Female dependence upon men extends beyond the need for protection against violence into more subtle areas. A woman without a man is subject to social disapproval, as Sally Wentworth's *Liberated Lady* discovers when she goes into a bar by herself to have a drink and is confronted with stares and speculation. When a man tries to pick her up, she is forced to say: "'Sorry, I'm waiting for my boyfriend,'" which makes everything all right with him and the rest of the bar patrons.[15] Clenching her teeth in anger, she gives up and leaves. Her freedom of movement in the world had been curtailed and she resents it.

Harlequins' insights into the manifestations of sexism in our society offer readers a glimpse of feminist theories that more fully describe that sexism. The heroine who deplores the low status of women's domestic labour, for example, echoes Margaret Benston's observations on the consequences of performing socially essential but unpaid labour in the home.[16] The heroine who has to invent a male companion for legitimacy is dealing with the heterosexist pressures analyzed by Adrienne Rich.[17] Feminist theories go far beyond Harlequins in their attempts to explain the origins of sexism but the romances have at least begun to acknowledge the existence of sexism, which is particularly evident in two specific areas – the workplace and in love relationships.

* * *

Heroines who are in stereotypically feminine occupations are aware that they are secretaries and nurses not out of their own burning ambition to be secretaries and nurses but because these are acceptable jobs for women that they have been encouraged or forced to enter. One heroine, a pianist and music teacher, decries the unfair process of occupational selection by gender in the example of a brilliant young working-class student who is drastically hampered by her parents, who show no interest in her work:

> What money there was, was being reserved for their son. The boy was their pride, bright at school, good at sport. In another year, he would be ready to go to university. Paying more money out on Jenny was unthinkable. She was destined, like every other girl, to become a receptionist or a typist like her mother had been.[18]

The heroine, aware that Jenny's class background as well as her gender will work against her, adopts her as a protégé and through much effort, political manipulation and persuasion, manages to get her star pupil accepted on scholarship into a prestigious music academy. Thus, there is encouragement for ambitious women alongside the critical observation that the race for education and jobs is rigged in favour of men.

In some cases, heroines have to struggle against traditional sex roles to be able to work at all. In *Return to Lanmore,* the heroine has to break off with her disapproving grandfather, whom she loves more than anything else in the world, in order to enter medical school. An old-fashioned man, he forbids her to go to school, maintaining that "'The women in our family have never needed to work. The idea's ridiculous.'"[19] Her violation is doubly unacceptable because she is not only planning to work but in a male-dominated occupation. She continues despite his objections and ultimately, is rewarded for her action. She gets her medical degree, is reunited with her grandfather who is secretly proud of her, and wins the hero as well. In both of these cases, Harlequins positively reinforce women or girls who break out of traditional sex-role limitations.

The heroines who escape woman-dominated occupations do not have an easy time of it. They are forced either to plea with or to threaten male employers for a chance to do their work:

> "Look," she pressed on ..., "I'm a professional, Dr. Ryder. I've come a very long way to do a job, and do it well. I would like you to extend me the courtesy of allowing me to prove that I can do just that. I do not need, nor do I want, to be treated as anything other than a completely equal coworker."[20]

> "... may I remind you of the Sex Discrimination Act? You have accepted my application on the basis of my experience and qualifications. The only reason you've given me for wanting to change your mind is because I'm a woman. I would say that made a perfect example of discrimination to place before an industrial tribunal, wouldn't you?"[21]

Once they have the job, they are conscious of being on trial in a man's world and are aware that they have to be very good – in fact, above reproach – to keep their jobs. Thus, when a heroine who is the lead singer in a band has a bad afternoon and criticizes the musicians, she feels that she must apologize and take them all out for lunch: "She was a lone woman working in a male-dominated environment, and the last thing she needed was to earn the reputation of being a temperamental bitch."[22] These examples are accurate reflections of the performance pressures and discrimination faced by women in non-traditional occupations in our society. Harlequins do not shirk from describing the difficulties women experience when they decide to pursue challenging careers in fields formerly closed to them.

This realistic approach is supplemented by the optimism that occupational barriers are not insurmountable. In these stories, assertiveness pays off for the heroines, who achieve interesting work and loving men, in contrast to the cost passive femininity extracts from the traditional rival women, who increasingly sound like the following:

> "I'm only working until I can find some lovely man to support me." She accompanied these words with a wistful look in Philip's direction. Though Nell rather despised fluffy, silly little girls, she couldn't help feeling sorry for Bobbie. If she was in love with Philip she was almost certainly in for heartbreak. Brilliant successful men were apt to demand more than just a pretty face.[23]

Sure enough, Philip chooses the plucky heroine.

More frequently than before, heroines are allowed to have both careers and marriage, in accordance with their stated desires. More heroines say they want to combine careers and marriage than those who actually do it but Harlequins no longer assume that a woman will automatically give up her job upon marriage. If a heroine does abandon the labour force, an explanation is necessary, an explanation usually couched in terms of love for husband and children or for freedom. In these cases, it is clear that she *chooses* not to participate in the labour force; she is not forced out by the failure to make it on her own. While being a full-time wife and mother is still considered to be a viable option, heroines increasingly want to keep their jobs after marriage. One heroine, observing a friend's marriage thinks:

> She had a brain, she wanted to use it, and if that meant she could never have the ideal marriage Melanie seemed to have then that was the way it was going to be. Shopping, seeing friends, and organising a household for her husband's pleasure and comfort was not something she could settle for in her life.[24]

Studies done nearly a decade ago found that the majority of college women envisioned dual career marriages for themselves. Only 5 percent favoured the traditional pattern of an employed husband and nonemployed wife.[25] Obviously Harlequins have lagged behind on this issue but the change evident in the romances moves them closer to a more positive and realistic portrayal of women's personal goals.

* * *

The consciousness of sexism and the desire for full, equal participation that are emerging in Harlequins' portrayals of women and work are also evident in their portrayals of women and love relationships. New heroines refuse to accept male dominance as right or natural. They inform their intended husbands that they will not be docile slaves, recognizing that subordination generates resentment rather than love. In *For Love of a Pagan,* for example, the hero forces the heroine to admit he is her master during love-making but her submission does not last very long:

> ... She would love him till she died, but that did not mean that she was willing to make a complete slave of herself.... She recalled with a sudden flush of humiliation her admission that he was her master ... after he had coerced her, ordered her to admit it.... Well, she had known she

would be angry later and she was angry! Never again would he force words like that from her lips! Who did he think he was – a god![26]

If the heroines refuse to play slave to his god, they also refuse to play goddess to his slave. They do not want a role reversal or a return to the courtly love of the middle ages. As one heroine puts it: "'I always considered the cult of courtly love was most immoral. I should hate to be stuck up on a pedestal and worshipped and have poems written to my eyebrows.'"[27]

The new heroines dream of a different type of relationship – one based on mutual respect, vulnerability and trust. Husbands and wives are expected to share their lives but they are also expected to maintain their individuality. Thus, a heroine expresses her desire for a more flexible relationship than has been the case in most Harlequins: "'What I should like is to have what my parents enjoyed: separate professional lives, and a shared private life.'"[28] Compare this to the claustrophobic ideal in the following Harlequins, published ten years earlier:

> "Love is doing things together, forgiving each other, loving the other so much that when he is miserable, you're miserable too, when he's happy so are you, if one of you treads on a nail the other's foot hurts.[29]
>
> "All I know is that when you fall in love ... you just love – and want, naturally, to spend every minute of the rest of your lives together."[30]

Some of the recent Harlequins, therefore, have progressed towards valuing more equal and realistic relationships that free both women and men from the impossible expectations traditionally associated with romantic marriage.

Equality means a more assertive sexual role for women. Heroines increasingly question the sexual double standard and recognize that they have been victimized by it: "'Men have organized the world for their own convenience for years. They made the laws, moral and otherwise, and it was men who sold women the idea that sexual desire is okay for a man but shameful for a woman.'"[31] As they rebel against these strictures, heroines are more likely to be sexually responsive. Cool and controlled on the outside, heroines are sensuous beings on the inside, and many a Harlequin describes the heroine's transformation from ice maiden to fiery seductress.

This transformation is the painful but ultimately joyful reunification of the mind / body split that afflicts heroines. At the beginning of the romances, heroines live almost totally in their heads and keep their bodies rigidly in control. Not surprisingly, when they meet the heroes and sexually respond to them, they experience the new sensations of their bodies as an alien experience – the body as traitor. Harlequins are very explicit about the mind/body split:

> ... the effort of trying to appear cool and unaware of him had already seriously depleted her small reserves of self-control. It was as though after years of being subordinate to her mind, her body had finally thrown off its yoke, making its own needs and desires all too plain.[32]

By the end of the romances, heroines learn to acknowledge and accept their bodies as an integral part of their selves. They are united at last: "She knew now that neither her heart nor her body had betrayed her, after all, in urging her to love this man."[33]

The focus on this split in Harlequin heroines reflects the dualism in our culture that has been promulgated most widely by Christianity. Believing that the soul is sacred and the body profane, this tradition encourages people to repress their bodily needs to focus on their spiritual ones. The injunction that "it is better to marry than to burn" was a grudging recognition that people are sexual and an admonition that if they must express their sexuality, they should do so within the limited context of marriage. Most churches have moved away from the extreme puritanical positions that characterized them in the past but the belief that the body is suspect still pervades our society.

This belief especially affects women because there has traditionally been more social pressure on them to suppress their sexuality. In addition, women have been taught to treat their bodies as objects to be moulded into the acceptable fashion no matter how harmful or unnatural that fashion may be. The discussion of women's alienation from their bodies is an important theme in women's movement literature. Feminists have encouraged women to trust their bodies, to learn to be at home in them and to listen to what their bodies are telling them. Harlequin romances now preach the same message to their readers! *Ms* magazine, in an article by Martha Nelson that is mainly critical in tone, sees some value in the books on this score.[34]

Heroines are not only responding, they are also initiating sexual encounters with more frequency. Even when unmarried, a heroine may seduce the hero, stay the night with him and ask him to marry her. Ironically their new responsiveness and their newly won prerogative to initiate sex means that, like men, they must face the possibility of rejection. Heroines now experience the sexual frustration of being "teased" by men. They have to handle the emotional devastation of being rejected when they have made themselves most vulnerable and exposed; they must deal with men who use access to their bodies as a tool for negotiation.

Some analysts like Mariam Frenier interpret this role reversal – female sexual arousal and male withdrawal – to be repression against women. She argues that women's sexuality is perceived to be dangerous and that the more it is manifested, the more it seems to be out of control and the more that it must be controlled; hence, "the heroines of sexy Harlequins are undermined in every possible way ..."[35]

This reading of Harlequins has some merit, as I pointed out in Chapter Five. However, the role reversal can also be seen as the beginning of the equal distribution of sexual power between the sexes. Traditionally women's source of power in society and in Harlequins resulted from the suppression of their sexuality; they bartered their bodies for marriage. Their power cost them their sexuality but gave them some economic security and emotional control over men. With the advent of the women's movement and new attitudes towards sexuality, which have encouraged women to be sexually responsive and assertive, this aspect of women's power has been eroded. Whereas in the earlier romances and society, women could bargain with but not enjoy sex, now both sexes can initiate and enjoy sex. Part of the trade-off involved in this change is that women become more vulnerable than before. It is difficult for women to take additional risks while giving up what little power they have, especially considering men have not yet taken on equal responsibilities for emotional support, housekeeping and childrearing. Harlequins show heroes and heroines moving closer to a middle ground in all these areas.

As already discussed, heroines have gained more extensive and rewarding participation in the labour force. With the confidence that they can make it on their own, they do not have to depend on men to provide them with a living. Thus, one heroine turns down a proposal of marriage from a wealthy rival man without a qualm: "That he offered her every luxury meant nothing to Bianca. Old-fashioned in certain ways, but modern in others, she had never thought of marriage as a meal-ticket." Later she comments that: "'Any luxuries I happen to fancy I'm quite capable of earning myself.'"[36] Since economic power is one of the most crucial determinants of marital power, heroines are better off today than they have ever been.

Another area in which heroines have made great strides is in the support networks available to them. In an earlier chapter I noted that increasingly, heroines have women friends whom they value and with whom they interact on a regular basis, even after marriage. This bond is portrayed to be a strong one, sometimes even outweighing the masculine-feminine one: "'No matter how different the cultures, women share a common bond in their feeling capacity and men share a common bond in their lack of understanding of women.'"[37] When heroines are in trouble, they frequently turn to a woman friend who is wise, understanding and supportive. Relationships between women friends are portrayed to be warm, intimate ties, which may be less intense but no less necessary than the male-female relationship. Dair Gillespie has cited social contacts outside marriage as a source of power within marriage and more and more heroines have this source of power available to them,[38] meaning they do not have to rely exclusively on the heroes.

Willard Waller talks about an additional source of power: "the principle of least interest."[39] Very simply, this concept refers to the fact that the person who is least interested in maintaining the relationship has the most power because he or she can more easily risk losing the relationship. The person least in love can control the rules by saying to the person who loves the most, "If you don't like it, leave," or they can walk out themselves. Heroines are very much in love with the heroes but some of them have reached the point of realizing that self-preservation takes precedence over their love:

> It was not an easy decision to make; to walk out on the only man she would ever love, but pride dictated that she could not continue living with him under these circumstances. She refused to be his plaything; a toy he could discard when it suited him, and that left her with only one thing to do. She had to go away ...[40]

Even Harlequin heroines slam the door these days.

Tania Modleski points out that this act is one of revenge, a childish fantasy of making those who have power over us sorry that they were so mean.[41] Yet the ability to leave a bad relationship is also evidence of the heroine's new maturity and independence. In addition, the act of leaving gives her power in the relationship because heroes love the heroines so much they cannot risk losing them. Love equalizes the power balance between the man and woman. Sometimes the balance is tipped in favour of the heroines, as in this romance in which the hero confesses:

> "... when I thought you'd gone again, I was ready to grovel. I didn't care if you hated me anymore, just as long as I found you and you agreed to stay.... I was ready to agree to any terms you cared to dictate."[42]

This portrayal is part fantasy, part realism: love does *not* make social inequality go away, but it does cushion the inequality within a given relationship. Significantly, the book ends with the hero's declaration of undying love, which is not mere romantic twaddle because it is also a declaration of undying equality!

* * *

Obviously much of the new heroine's happiness and equality hinges on the development of the hero into a "new male." Just as heroines have evolved into more balanced individuals, combining their traditional sensitivity with new-found independence, so heroes have become more balanced by combining their traditional strength with new-found emotionality and vulnerability.

Authors convey this vulnerability through a number of oft-repeated phrases the reader quickly learns to recognize: when the hero has heard bad news or the heroine is cruel to him, he flinches as if struck; he turns white and the lines at the corner of his mouth are etched more deeply than usual; his eyes are marked with pain; he may sway on his feet or cry. Most heroines initially doubt their perceptions of the heroes' vulnerability:

> Opening her eyes, she saw for an instant how bleak his features were, how pain-filled his eyes, before a mask of cold anger closed over his face, obliterating any other emotion so she wondered if she had imagined that fleeting agony.[43]

The reader knows that what she saw was indeed pain and eventually the heroine does too: "... what startled her was the discovery that his exterior look of hardness wasn't proof that he was a hardened man."[44] The hero, formerly an unfathomable, intimidating "man of steel" begins to show more of his feelings, creating the possibility of equality between him and the heroine.

New heroes have also begun to take on domestic tasks that were previously women-only chores, such as cooking and serving food, doing dishes, folding clothes and, especially, taking care of children. One hero boasts: "'You're not marrying a helpless nitwit, darling. I can look after you and myself too,'"[45] and for once he does not mean that he earns enough money to support a family and a maid, but that he can fend for himself in the kitchen. Heroines are as surprised by the new hero's domesticity as they are by his emotionality: "It still amazed her that, even in these days of sex liberation, he was more meticulous than the most houseproud woman."[46] But they quickly adjust to this change. After exposure to the domestically self-sufficient heroes, heroines realize "how agreeable it must be to live with a man who could keep his clothes clean and mended, and was not dependent on a woman always to attend to them for him ..."[47] Just as helpless feminine rivals bore the heroes, helpless masculine rivals now irritate the heroines:

> After supper, while the two men chatted, she cleared the table, washed the dishes and made up the sofa-bed....Michael could see her doing this last, but he didn't offer to help. She had always known that he was an extremely undomesticated man, partly because he had a widowed mother who delighted in doing his laundry when he went home for the weekends, and who had even been known to come to London for a day's shopping and spend half of it tidying his flat. But now, in light of her association with Joe ..., she found his incompetence irritating.[48]

Some progress has been made from the days when the heroes expected the heroines to be responsible for all the domestic labour and the heroines found masculine domesticity threatening.

Another area in which heroes have made concessions is work commitment. In the new romances, heroes have careers that are important to them. But, like the heroines, they learn to subordinate them to love and marriage in order to be happy. Mutual over-commitment to a career is frequently the obstacle between the hero and heroine and *both* must give up some of their ambition to be united. She gives up the most but increasingly he must make some concessions. For example, in *Passionate Stranger,* the heroine, a fabric designer, quits her full-time job because "suddenly it was not important any more," but the hero, a musician, also changes his thinking about his career:

> "... I have had plenty of time to think ... about you mostly ... but also

about me, and I have discovered that although performing music in public is still very necessary to me it isn't more important to me than you are. It doesn't come first with me any more. You do."[49]

This hero is not alone in changing his priorities. In *Rimmer's Way,* the heroine is warned not to get involved with the hero because all he cares about is his ranch. By the end of the story, the hero is prepared to completely abandon the ranch if she doesn't want to stay there:

"Damn and blast the land!" exploded Cal. "Wherever you are will be home to me. I only wish you had taken to the ranch because it's part of me, but it's not worth losing you. Nothing is worth that much!"[50]

These new heroes have become more willing to subordinate their work to their wives and children than they have been in the past.

All of these changes indicate an evolution in Harlequins' conception of an "ideal man" from a dominant, unfeeling, uncompromising breadwinner to a sensitive human being who can be a loving friend. A heroine expects the hero to share her interests in music or literature, to have a good sense of humour and an understanding of what it means to be a woman in a rapidly changing world, to be intelligent, supportive and a good father.[51]

Although the hero has acquired these "softer" qualities, he has retained his strength, which has been redefined to mean nonthreatening self-confidence, flexibility and humility. For example, one test of whether a man is up to hero status is if he is strong enough to accept the heroine's occupational success. Both the heroines in *Liberated Lady* and *Flying High* have had the experience of going with men who could not handle their achievements. Once the heroines advanced in their careers, the relationships ended. The narrator of *Liberated Lady* describes the process of dissolution:

And then she had been promoted ahead of her fiance. He had laughed at first, passing it off as just a fluke, only half-jokingly saying that she must have fluttered her eyelashes at the boss, but they both knew well enough that in advertising, you only get promotions through merit, and something died in their relationship. Shortly after she received a second promotion he went out and spent their joint savings on a power-boat. Sara had known then that it was over.[52]

Buying a power boat is a rather humourous example of what Herb Goldberg calls "macho-psychotic behaviour" – senseless and destructive acts that show the world that the men are big, tough and powerful.[53]

Recognizing the weakness that lies behind the macho facade, a heroine rejects this type of man even as he rejects her: "Not that she wanted, needed, the outdated *macho* image that had made women slaves to their domineering husbands in times past. Her preference would be for a man as confident of his maleness as she was of her femininity ..."[54] In contrast to the rival men, therefore, the hero is so self-confident that he can accept the heroine's accomplishments. Thus, when one heroine tells her affianced hero that she's always assumed that, with the right man, she would have both children and her work, he replies: " 'You do, I believe, have the right man.' "[55]

The new hero's strength also means that he can admit he is wrong. Heroes who were opposed to having heroines work with them admit that the women proved to be competent, even brilliant; heroes who had fixed ideas of a woman's place in society do a complete turnabout and say that they have been stupid; heroes who have mistreated the heroines abase themselves and beg for forgiveness. The new hero is able to admit that he is a frog in prince's clothing:

> "Once upon a time I used to dream about a girl like you, someone pretty and spirited, who would need me as much as I needed her. Now I find her and I'm the one who's wrong. In this tale the prince has turned into a frog.... I'm sorry."[56]

A striking example of this new hero and a glimpse of the incorporation of sometimes grim reality in Harlequins takes place in Daphne Clair's *The Loving Trap*. Although Harlequins have steered away from discussing serious social and personal problems in the past, in this romance the heroine is a woman who has been gang-raped as an adolescent. She falls in love with and marries the hero but does not tell him about the rape. On the honeymoon, she tenses up whenever he comes near her and for a while he is patient but when she shows no signs of loosening up, he becomes angry and nearly forces himself on her. Before he can do so, she cries out bitterly that he is not "the first," which stops him cold. She tells him the story and anxiously awaits his response:

> She looked up briefly, then, and saw what she had dreaded. His face was pale, and there was a tight look of fury about his mouth and a savage anger in his eyes. And something else – distaste, disgust.[57]

She cannot bear to live with him knowing that he is repulsed by her because of her "sordid" past, so she leaves. One rainy night some time later, she is rescuing a stranded kitten from her dark back yard when a male figure comes towards her. She screams in terror and tries to run away until the hero identifies himself. He cries and says shakily: "'Kyla, don't run from me, *please* don't. I'll never hurt you, never again. I promise darling. I promise.'"[58] When they go inside to talk about their marriage, he asks her to come back to him, promising that he would never make love to her against her will: "'I don't look forward to a *platonic* marriage. But if it's all you can take, I'll settle for that.'"[59] She tells him she doesn't understand why he still wants her when she saw how she disgusted him. He is thunderstruck: "'Must I add *that* to everything else I've done to you?'" he mutters, and then he explains his reaction:

> "When you told me what had happened to you, I felt – violent. I wanted to track them down and smash them with my bare hands, for what they'd done to you. And then – it dawned on me that I'd just damn near raped you myself and that made me about on a level with them. I was disgusted, all right – sick with it. But never with you. I despised *myself*, Kyla, not you!"[60]

This is indeed a new hero who realizes that his love does not make his behaviour magically acceptable and that love does not excuse brutality.

The Loving Trap is also an example of the increasing criticism of sexual violence found in Harlequins. In the last chapter, I discussed the romanticization of sexual violence and sexual harassment which is fairly common in recent romances, but alongside the romanticization a deliberate repudiation of violence is developing. Charlotte Lamb's *A Violation* is one of the first Harlequins to portray, during the course of the story, a nonromanticized rape and its devastating aftereffects. The author discusses her intent:

> I wanted to write a positive book, showing how a woman can survive a brutal act of violence, cope with her own fear and depression after it and emerge stronger, able to love again, trust again, risk a relationship with a man again.[61]

As part of her recovery from the rape, the heroine ends her relationship with the rival man, whose attitude towards her is almost as dehumanizing as the rapist's act, and is able to begin a relationship with the hero, who is more understanding.

In many recent Harlequins, the author is careful to inform the reader that the hero is not the type of man who rapes or hits women. Some of the standard portrayals of heroes, which seem to be merely reinforcements of traditional sex roles, can be reinterpreted in the light of this trend. Thus, the emphasis on the hero's self-confidence, which borders on arrogance, and his overwhelming sexual magnetism can be reassuring signs that he *does not have to* strike out at women who cross him, *does not have to* take women against their will because he is not a weak, easily threatened man who has no other alternative but violence. Similarly, the incidents where the hero sexually teases the heroine can been seen, not just as the exertion of power, but as an encouraging indication that the hero is a man strong enough to hold even his most "primitive" emotions in check.

The new hero, increasingly sensitized to issues of power and violence, has the strength to step back and let the heroine decide what she wants. He is willing to trust her to decide what is best for her; he controls himself in order to avoid controlling her. He may even go out of his way to ensure that she does not have to marry him and that she has other alternatives. In *Yours With Love,* the hero bows out of the heroine's life to give her time to go to school, find a job and go out with other men because he realizes that he has been taking over her life. He never does approach her again; she must go to him on her own accord, but his action pays off for both of them:

> "It couldn't," said Virginia, "have been very easy for *you.*"
> "Easy!" He laughed slightly, and then to her dismay, she felt him shudder. "No, it wasn't easy. But it was the right thing. And strangely enough, for the first time in my life, I cared very deeply what the right thing was."
> "Jason, I think if I hadn't loved you before, I should love you now."[62]

Harlequins exhibit a surprising complexity and even, in some cases, an emerging feminism in these positive portrayals of women, work, love and marriage. Traditional sex roles are breaking down in romances as heroines become more assertive and heroes become more emotional. As these characters converge, the dominant/submissive relationships between men and women traditionally valued in romance are increasingly displaced by the possibility of more equal relationships.

Readers have responded positively to the changes in romances by buying more than ever. The next chapter will examine who reads romances and why they read them.

*

CHAPTER SEVEN

THE GRAND PASSION
OF PRACTICAL PEOPLE

... no matter how vulgarized the sentimental myth may have become, no matter how smugly we snicker at it, we are somehow still its victims and beneficiaries.

Leslie Fiedler
Love and Death in the American Novel

People say that life is the thing, but I prefer reading.

Logan Pearsall Smith
Afterthoughts

The interest in the messages of romances is ultimately linked to concern about the receivers of these messages. Three major questions usually arise in the course of this concern. First, who reads romances? Little old ladies with blue-grey hair? Harried housewives with several whining children tugging at their skirts? Starry-eyed, impressionable young girls? A dozen stereotypes come to mind when one mentions romance readers and a dozen more when one speculates about why women read romances. Close on the heels of this concern is the even more alarming speculation about the effect of romances on readers. These three questions – who reads romances, why and with what effect – are crucial ones to address for an understanding of their popularity and significance. In order to achieve this understanding, we must set aside the stereotypes to take a fresh look at romance readers.

* * *

Romance readers are spread throughout the female population. The more than twenty million women who read romances are a widely diffuse group of individuals; no stereotype comes close to describing their diversity. Peter Mann, who conducted two surveys of Harlequin's British readers, one in 1968 with 2,788 readers and another in 1973 with 2,000 respondents, concludes:

> After nearly five years of contact with romantic novels I now feel that is is possible to write with some assurance about their readers. If one may sum up in a word, they are "Everywoman" ...[1]

Mann found that a third of readers were full-time housewives, 30 percent were married women with either full-time or part-time jobs and 22 percent were unmarried women with jobs. The rest were either retired or full-time students. Nearly three-quarters of the women who were employed worked in clerical or sales occupations.[2]

Consumer research surveys conducted by Harlequin Enterprises reiterate Mann's findings that in North America, as in England, romance readers are scattered throughout the population. The company has constructed profiles of the North American English-speaking female population, the Harlequin reading population and the Harlequin buying population. (Company officials estimate that there are approximately twice as many readers as buyers due to extensive borrowing of books; this is typical of the paperback industry.) According to Harlequin's sales manager, the profiles of these three groups are identical for characteristics like age, family income, employment status and geographical location. For example, he said that if 22 percent of the female population is between the ages of 25 and 34, then 22 percent of the Harlequin reading population is between the ages of 25 and 34. The only difference he cited was that the number of Harlequin readers graduating from college is about 2 percent lower than the national average. Otherwise, as phrased by company officials, "To make a long story short, our reader is Mrs. Johnny Q. Public or Mrs. Average America." Both Mann and Harlequin Enterprises emphasize the broad range of romance readers.

There are some variations in reader characteristics revealed by consumer research surveys done by other publishers. Silhouette indicates that its average reader is in her early thirties, is married, employed and has some college education. Her median family income is $22,000. *The Romantic Times,* on the basis of 1,000 responses, found that the average romance reader is about forty. A survey by Barbara Cartland's *World of Romance* magazine established the median age of readers at thirty-six. Almost 60 percent of the readers in that sample were employed and their family income (determined eighteen months before the Silhouette figures were taken) was $17,200.[3] A national study of 600 readers by Carol Thurston found that 40 percent of her sample were employed full-time and nearly half of them had some college education.[4] It is difficult to compare these studies since publishing companies are very secretive about their consumer research projects and they do not use uniform measurements. Some reports describe an average reader while others look at a range of readers. Frequently reports do not define crucial terms like "employed," which further restrict comparisons and inferences. Nevertheless, studies of romance readers overwhelmingly indicate that they are a diverse population that defies stereotyping. Carol Thurston, like Harlequin Enterprises, concludes that the romance reader can be every woman and any woman: "I found that they mirror the general population in age, education, and marital and socioeconomic status."[5]

The group of women I interviewed fit the picture of diverse readership drawn by these large studies.[6] I talked to women who ranged in age from eighteen to seventy-six years old; who ranged in educational attainment from grade three to college; who ranged in ethnic background from Polish to British, Trinidadian to Italian; who ranged in their family size from no children to fourteen. These readers were single, married and widowed women who had worked as factory workers, teachers, cocktail waitresses, housewives and students. The common denominator that linked my readers to other surveys is that uniformly women who read romances identify themselves as "readers." They have an ongoing love affair with books. Romances predominate but they also read westerns, mysteries, historical novels, travel books, best sellers, nonfiction, newspapers and magazines. Reading is their main leisure activity; they are not dedicated television watchers.

During their leisure time, they manage to read enormous numbers of books. According to a 1976 Harlequin advertising campaign: "The average Harlequin reader buys 72 of our books each year."[7] This North American rate is higher than the British consumption of forty-eight to sixty books a year reported by Mann but does not even come close to the figures reported by Rosemary Guiley in *Love*

Lines: "... 'light' readers of romance read up to twenty-five books a *month,* and 'heavy' readers devour eighty or more ..."[8] Silhouette maintains that its average reader buys thirty books a month.[9]

The number of books read by the women I interviewed depends on a variety of factors such as health, family demands, occupational demands and seasons of the year. The "heaviest" reader reads sixty Harlequins a month while the woman who reads the least reads only two a month. By Guiley's standards, most of the women I talked with would be defined as "light" readers, reading an average of between twelve and sixteen Harlequins a month. Compared to the non-reading general public however, even the "light" romance readers that I interviewed are readers indeed.

Women not only read, they also collect romances. Hundreds of women replied to a Harlequin collector's contest. Some 225 readers had more than 1,500 Harlequins while the "winner" had 2,465 Harlequins in her collection. These women spend hours not only reading ("one reader realizes that she had put in 5,724 hours"[10]) and re-reading ("'I have read some of the books as many as ten times'"[11]), but also organizing their collections – arranging their bookshelves, filing and cross-filing index cards on the books and working out rating systems. The women I interviewed were not primarily collectors; most of them exchange the books they have read for others. This is probably typical of the majority of readers; however, I talked to four women who have collections of 150 books or more and one of these has over 1,000.

Since there are are more readers than buyers and since many readers exchange their books for new ones, they obviously obtain their books from sources other than Harlequin Enterprises. One key source is other women. Many new readers are introduced to romances by established readers, as is true of over two-thirds of the group I interviewed. This romance network obviously spans the generation gap; readers tell of grandmothers, mothers, daughters, sisters and aunts who are romance fans. Women also get their books from used bookstores, from garage sales, through contacts in card, bingo and ceramic clubs and classes, and from libraries. Where women obtain their Harlequins seems to depend on the extent of the woman's interest in romances, the amount of time and money she can spend, her health, age and geographical location. Elderly or bedridden women who cannot easily get to stores, women who live in remote areas, committed readers who cannot stand to wait for the monthly releases and who are afraid they will miss some of the titles, and women who are too busy to shop for Harlequins on the stands come to rely on the company's subscription and mail-order service. For others who have the time and energy or those who cannot afford to buy new Harlequins, hunting for secondhand romances is a hobby, part of the pleasure of reading the books.

As readers responded to my questions about their source and use of Harlequins, it became evident that they could be divided into three basic groups which cross age, race, marital status and occupational lines. These groups are based on readers' attachment to romances and include the keen, casual and critical reader.

The keen reader is a woman who proudly declares she is "hooked" on Harlequins. She may own a collection of them and be conversant about authors' styles, the differences between various romance lines and trends in the genre. She is largely dependent upon romances for entertainment and her "addiction" may interfere with her work or relationships. The following woman is an example of a keen reader:

> I was introduced to your marvelous books at our local library. I read them all and started buying out the stock at the drug store before I joined your club. I cannot get enough of them!
>
> The children dread the day the books arrive because I sit right down and go through them, sometimes into the night. My husband has declared me an addict.[12]

Keen readers constitute a minority of the romance reading population. About half of the women I talked with agreed that they could be considered to be "hooked" on Harlequins but they seemed to use the term lightly. Only two women genuinely fit this category. One of the keen readers was a single, twenty-three-year-old Black woman from Trinidad who worked as a visiting homemaker. She had just discovered Harlequins and told me that: "whereas normally I would look to go out, now I don't. I prefer to stay at home and read. I stay home all the time and read every spare moment that I have, that's what I do." Harlequins had affected her relationships with men: "You find that whenever you meet a guy, you kind of measure him up and if you find him wanting, like what Mr. Harlequin is, then you say, 'He's not for me.' There's a better guy along, so you don't pay him very much attention." The other keen reader was a thirty-eight-year-old housewife and mother of a teenage daughter. This woman read sixty Harlequins a month. Since it took her about four hours to read one, she spent fifty-six hours a week reading romances. Keen readers are the delight of the romance industry and the horror of critics who are rightly concerned about the detrimental role romances play in these readers' lives.

The second category is the casual reader, who constitutes the vast majority of Harlequin readers. She uses the books as a leisure activity that fits into her work schedule. Recognizing that Harlequins are fantasy, she expresses no desire to marry a Harlequin hero, who is seen as being too handsome, too rich, too perfect or just unreal. This woman is puzzled or amused when presented with the suggestion that romances might be bad for her. She feels fully in control of her romance reading.

The final category of readers, a very small minority, is the critical reader. This woman does not really approve of romances but she is drawn to them anyway. She is likely to have intellectual or political doubts about the romances so that when she reads them, she reads them against her better judgment. In some cases, she is able to mock them easily and be reassured about the soundness of her values. In other cases, however, her enduring fascination with images and ideas she opposes may confuse, frighten or depress her. She may be a keen reader who no longer enjoys her addiction to romances and feels trapped by her insatiable desire for more romances. Since this woman does not identify herself as a romance reader and may even hide her books if she keeps any in the house, she is difficult to study. Nevertheless, a careful analysis of the romance text and feedback from other readers can help us understand what attracts even reluctant readers to romantic fiction.

* * *

Both the number of readers and the number of romances they read call for an explanation. Why *do* women like romantic fiction? When I asked readers that question, the most common response was that the books were "light reading." Two-thirds of the women mention that they like Harlequins because they can "pick them up and put them down" with ease. The books are predictable, characters are immediately recognizable, and each book moves along at about the same pace. The reader knows when she opens a book a third, one-half or three-quarters of the way through approximately what has gone on and what will still unfold. Most critics dislike this aspect of Harlequins but it is precisely this feature that readers value. Obviously, an explanation of why readers like romances must include an explanation of why readers like formula fiction.

Formula fiction is easy to read. For busy women who consider themselves to be "readers," the accessibility of formula fiction enables them to read under difficult conditions. The advantage of formula fiction is particularly evident in the lives of two large groups of romance readers: full-time housewives / mothers and women employed in the labour force.

Employed women frequently take Harlequins to the job with them. One has only to ride the bus or subway during rush hour to see this is true. They sit down, open their purses and are instantly absorbed in the story until their stop, whereupon the books are closed and popped back into their purses. Women also read Harlequins on lunch and coffee breaks, a pattern that has been evident for a long time. A woman who worked in a box-making sweat shop in New York in 1905 described her fellow workers' infatuation with romances:

> Although we had a half hour, luncheon was swallowed quickly by most of the girls, eager to steal away to a sequestered bower among the boxes, there to lose themselves in paper-backed romance.... Promptly at half past twelve the awakening machinery called us back to the workaday world. Storybooks were tucked away and their entranced readers dragged themselves back to the machines and steaming pastepots, to dream and to talk as they worked ... of bankers and mill-owners who in fiction have wooed and won and honorably wedded just such poor toilers as they themselves.[13]

Why do women devote their commuting time and lunch hours to romance? One reason is that reading formula fiction allows women to be physically present but mentally absent. Erving Goffman has introduced the concept of "removal activities" to describe the tactics used by inmates of institutions to get through long, boring repetitive days.[14] Removal activities help time pass more quickly by making the practitioners temporarily forget where they are or even who they are while they are absorbed in some mindless yet engrossing activity. Goffman gives the examples of playing solitaire or daydreaming but he could well have cited reading romances. Harlequins are written in a fast-paced, easy-to-read style that makes reading them an effortless escape. Harlequin Enterprises plays on this by describing its romances as a woman's "disappearing act." Like inmates in an institution, women's freedom of movement and association are restricted by the structure of their working day and they engage in removal activities to get through the boring stretches. Commuting along the same route twice daily is monotonous "dead time" that Harlequin readers convert to more enjoyable reading time. Reading on a bus or subway serves a double function in that it also envelops the reader in a protective cocoon of privacy. The open book and the reader's averted eyes are messages to fellow passengers that the woman does not want to be disturbed. This message protects the reader from unwanted interactions with anyone who interprets a woman sitting alone as an invitation to a conversation or a proposition. Reading is, therefore, time out, time for self. As such, it is one of the few luxuries that many busy working women can afford to give themselves.

Harlequin's light formula also permits full-time housewives and mothers to read under difficult conditions – constant interruptions, tedious household chores, hectic coordination of the family's comings and goings, and the lack of adult companionship. Like employed women, housewives build short Harlequin reading periods into their working days when children nap, watch television or go to school. Reading is their way to take some time out. As one reader explained:

> I got into the habit, for instance, my kids would eat their lunch and they'd want to watch the Flintstones and that drives me right up the wall, eh? And on a day like this, I wouldn't mind sitting with my second cup of tea. It would be the first time I sat down since I got up and I look forward to it.

Women's working conditions in the home, therefore, partially dictate what they are able to read because it is difficult to read a complex or "deep" novel in short twenty-minute to a half-hour snatches of time. One young mother told me:

> I've always been a reader.... I could go through maybe four or five novels in a weekend, like hard-covered ones, thick ones, you know. And when I had the kids, I never could.... You can't get back into those books because I'm the type that once they pick up a book they can't put it down and nothing annoys me more than you've got to get supper on the table or someone's crying to have their diaper changed or something. So they're smaller, they're compact. They're light reading so that

I can put them down and pick them up, maybe a day or so later and I can remember it.

Harlequin's formula allows women to read under conditions not generally conducive to reading. A woman with several small children related:

Well, it does take you away from your dishes and your kids hollering at you. It gives you something to think of ... and you can put them down and you can come back to it.... you are kind of cornered by all these kids all day long and these bring in a new vocabulary at least. A Harlequin takes you away and you don't have to listen to your children.... You can have more patience with them if your mind is occupied someplace else.

Women's lives as housewives and mothers encourage this dispersal of concentration; they must deal with the fact that much of their work requires their physical presence but does not fully tap their mental capabilities. One of the ways women cope with this is to shut down mentally; rather than concentrating on the task at hand, they daydream. According to Ann Oakley, this response is a practical solution to their working conditions:

All these strands of thought fulfill a latent function for the housewife. They enable her to get housework done; thinking about something else is a weapon deliberately employed in the attempt to combat boredom.... In this sense, daydreaming is purposeful – not merely a random response to a superfluity of mentally unoccupied time.[15]

Harlequins are ready-made daydreams that women use to help them function without succumbing to the stress of the daily routine.

Employed women and full-time housewives account for the majority of Harlequin readers. In addition, there are smaller groups of readers who also use Harlequins to fill in time. Elderly women, for example, who cannot get about easily and are largely confined to the home, women who are forced to be idle for health reasons, women whose children have left home and who are suddenly faced with large blocks of empty time, or women who are widowed and bereft of their husbands' companionship turn to Harlequins to take their minds off their troubles. As light reading, the romances blend easily into the most diverse range of readers' lives.

Women read Harlequins not only for escape but as a form of entertaining education. Half of the readers I talked with mentioned they like the different settings in Harlequins. For North American women, the settings, which have not usually featured North America, are foreign and "exotic." Readers often choose to read a specific romance on the basis of its setting. They feel that while they are enjoying themselves, they are also learning about other countries, the people and their customs. The "educational" aspect of the books is sometimes used by readers to justify their reading to outsiders or skeptics. One woman reported to *Harlequin* magazine that her family had Australian visitors and she was able to converse knowledgeably with them about Australia because she had read romances set there. She concluded: "I feel after last evening with our Aussie friends, my family will not rib me anymore when they see me reading my Harlequins ..."[16]

The knowledge acquired in Harlequins is usually stereotypical and superficial, consisting of trivia like the British use of "biscuits" and "jelly" rather than the North American terms, "cookies" and "jello." In some of the longer romances such as the SuperRomance series, however, authors have time to elaborate on settings. For example, in *River of Desire,* a SuperRomance by Abra Taylor, the heroine is making a television documentary about a small native tribe in the heart of Brazil and the reader is given a considerable amount of anthropological information.

Readers also learn language from romances. An Italian-born woman told me that Harlequins helped her learn and improve her English. Peter Mann has reported similar cases in his studies. According to other readers, school-age girls use Harlequins as material for book reports and develop their reading and writing skills in the process. This function of romance reading prompted a *Wall Street Journal* editorial by Vermont Royster, who learned that an exclusive American private school downgraded applicants if they confessed they read romances. He recalled his own boyhood addiction to "trash" like Tom Swift and the Rover Boys, which began his lifetime habit of reading and concluded: "If the girls will just read, let them read."[17]

Because Harlequins glamourize settings, fashion, food and people, the vocabulary used is fairly extensive. For example, in a romance, one does not go out to mow the lawn, one ventures forth to trim the verdant sward! This overblown language justifiably comes under attack from literary critics but it is the traditional romance writing style that is used to evoke glamour and excitement, an essential aspect of popular formula fiction.

Harlequins also give their readers a social network by providing them with a symbolic and sometimes real community of friends. Women write that they consider the books, the characters and the company and its staff to be their friends. Harlequin and its authors, of course, do everything in their power to play up this image. Editors and authors adopt a folksy tone when they deal with the public and reader parties are an obvious attempt to heighten readers' sense of involvement with the company. All of these "friends" form what one might term a "pseudo-community" because one of the necessary characteristics that defines a real community – face-to-face interaction – is missing.

Sometimes women do come in contact with other readers and Harlequins provide a topic of conversation. When I asked readers whether they talked to anyone about Harlequins, just over half said they did but their conversations seemed to be brief. Most women probably do not so much discuss individual Harlequins as simply exchange them. This romance swapping takes place as part of neighbouring or family relationships. I interviewed one woman who insisted on taking me to the house of a friend. I found out that running back and forth with the books was a regular part of their routine. Exchanging Harlequins gives women an excuse to get out of the house and to visit with others.

There is nothing unique about romances that fosters social interaction among users. All forms of popular culture, whether it be soaps, sports or crafts, furnish people with common experiences that form a bond between them. Romances are no exception and readers value them for this function.

Readers like the formula fiction aspect of Harlequins for one additional reason. The tight editorial control that results in romance uniformity means that women know they are making a good consumer choice when they buy Harlequins. One reader told me: "They're very predictable, which is good too, isn't it? You know what you're buying." Women need not worry that they are buying an unknown quantity which they may discover they dislike, making their purchase a waste of money. Like fast food franchises and hotel chains around the world, Harlequins are dependable choices. They are also cheap compared to most forms of entertainment, especially if the reader buys them secondhand. Compare the price of a new Harlequin ($2 to $2.50) to the price of a movie, pop and popcorn. One can quickly see the economic advantages of curling up with a romance.

Women read formula fiction to meet their needs for cheap entertainment, sociability, easy education and predictable plots that allow one to be interrupted without losing track of the story. We must now attempt to understand why, out of the choices of popular fiction available to them, women prefer reading romances.

* * *

If Harlequins are read as feminine defeats in which heroines abdicate responsibility for themselves to the nearest powerful male, extensive explanations are needed to tell us why so many women want to read about submission and defeat. Theorists who interpret the books this way explicitly believe that romance readers are masochistic. Tania Modleski criticizes this belief and argues in favour of a different perspective:

> The notion of "adaptation" is an important one, for it implies some sort of activity on the part of women, not just passive acceptance. In exploring female romantic fantasies, I want to look at the varied and complex strategies women use to adapt to circumscribed lives ... [18]

I agree that we must attempt to understand the dynamic interaction between women, their lives and romances. We must acknowledge that women who choose to read romances are not merely masochistic or the passive dupes of Harlequin Enterprises. We may not like many aspects of romances but our disagreements with the books do not allow us to make condescending judgments about the intelligence or normalcy of romance readers. These judgments are counterproductive, as Janet Patterson points out:

> The attempt to account for why women are attracted to a phenomena which is obviously sexist results more often than not in contempt for the readership rather than understanding of the significance of this literary culture. [19]

To make any sense out of romantic fantasies, we must try to understand their appeal from the perspective of the reader.

All available evidence indicates that readers perceive a romance's conclusion to be a happy ending – a victory, not a defeat. The desire to hear tales of adversity and triumph is universal and Harlequin readers are drawn to romances because, after 180 pages of struggle, the heroine emerges "a winner." Indeed it is this fantasy ending, in juxtaposition with the more realistic conflict that precedes it, that emotionally "hooks" readers. Harlequins' power and appeal lie in their ability to graphically pose and magically solve some of the problems that women must deal with in our society.

In Chapter Five, I criticized Harlequins' portrayal of women as a marginal labour force. Heroines frequently show little long-term or full-time commitment to their work and move in and out of the labour force at will. In reality, most women have to work out of financial need and even women who drop out of the labour force for a time to bear and raise children can expect to spend an average of twenty-six years in the labour force.[20] Although the majority of women want to hold jobs and although employment outside the home benefits women in many significant ways, working also adds to their problems. The hassles of finding good child care and the expense when one does, the juggling of time spent on the job, house-keeping and family, and the added costs of transportation, clothes and convenience products cause many women to wonder if having a job outside the home is worth the trouble. Employed wives and mothers are frequently physically and emotionally exhausted from trying to balance all the demands placed upon them. They may feel like failures because they don't have the time or energy to do a good job in all areas (perhaps in any area) of their lives. They are caught in the midst of role conflict and feel trapped by the lack of alternatives available to them to resolve that conflict. Their frustration is compounded by the fact that they are isolated in a few low-paid, low status occupations. They make substantial sacrifices in their personal lives for very little economic or social return.

Those women who escape the "pink collar ghetto" into the professions discover they have not escaped sexism. They quickly perceive the pressure to become "imitation men," to become hard-driving, aggressive and dominant, in order to succeed. The negative portrait of career women in Harlequins is partially a recognition of the price women pay when they must function in an emotionally repressive, male-dominated work world for which they are ill prepared by their sex-role socialization. Penalized financially if they do not adopt traditionally male patterns of interaction and penalized emotionally if they do, professional women are confronted with tough choices and no-win situations.

In contrast to the work-related problems in their lives, romance readers dream about the luxury of creative, challenging work, the luxury of being able to choose to work or not, the luxury of part-time work with flexible hours, the luxury of shared work that will bring them closer to their husbands. Similarly, in contrast to the financial insecurity, isolation and boring tasks women face in the home, romance readers dream about generous, wealthy husbands and housekeepers who provide companionship and lighten the work load. Their fantasies are an understandable, albeit extremely limited compensation for the lack of options in their lives. Women who read romances are fantasizing about freedom.

Harlequins' appeal is strengthened by the fact that women are socialized to value love relationships. The focus of the books – courtship and early marriage – has been shown to be one of the happiest periods of women's lives.[21] Harlequins emphasize the stage in women's life cycle during which they enjoy the greatest amount of freedom, independence, power, companionship and equality that they will have, at least until post-childrearing years. This is a stage women look forward to when they are young and enjoy retrospectively when they are older. It is understandable that women like to read about a period in their lives that involves the establishment of love relationships, a central part of their psychological makeup.

Examining women's realities also helps explain the persistence and appeal of the conflict between the nice heroine and the nasty rival woman. The heroine is not as beautiful as the rival woman but the rival, in spite of her beauty, does not win the hero. The reassuring message to readers is that men can see beyond superficial physical beauty to the beauty within, which they prefer. In contrast to this fantasy, men in reality indicate that a woman's physical attractiveness is an important determinant of whether they will go out with her or not. The importance of beauty, coupled with the shifting, stringent definitions of beauty in our society, means that most women are anxious about their appearances. Harlequins soothe this anxiety by making personality more important than beauty. The fantasy is made even more appealing because the hero honestly believes that the heroine is the sexiest, most fascinating woman alive, even though the heroine knows very well she is not. Harlequins give a voice to women's wishful thinking that either beauty would not count so much or that they themselves would be considered beautiful.

The portrayal of heroes as enigmatic, sensitive macho men is a key aspect of the Harlequin fantasy. Heroes are "inscrutable," in comparison to heroines, who are "transparent." These portrayals are rooted in traditional sex roles in our society. Jack Balswick and Charles Peek have referred to the modern North American male as "inexpressive" and studies show that men disclose less of themselves than women.[22] Taught to repress emotions and to hide vulnerability, men are enigmas for many women, who have been socialized to be the exact opposite. Women's uncertainty about what men are thinking or feeling is exacerbated by the fact that courtship is done in code. Women spend countless hours, individually and in friendship groups, trying to decipher the meanings of words, facial expressions, gestures and actions of the men with whom they are involved or want to be involved. Harlequins assure readers that all is well. If men would only speak, they would say, "I love you."

This message is particularly important to women, given the pervasive threat of sexual violence in our society. Without exception, studies of fear of crime reveal that women are more afraid of violence than men, and with good reason. Sexual violence has been increasing more rapidly than any other form of violent crime; some sources estimate that one in every three women will be raped during her lifetime.[23] Many of these rapes will be committed by men the victims know and trust. Wife abuse is another widespread form of violence against women that is characterized by betrayal of trust. The home is turned into a battleground more violent than the streets and the husband is transformed into a hateful enemy more dreaded than the furtive stranger.

Since women's relationships with men are a disturbing mixture of fear and attraction, love and hate, it is not surprising that these tensions surface in their literature. Readers can realistically identify with the heroine who silently pleads with the hero: "Go.... Don't you feel the vibrations in this room? There's anger here, but there's something sexual too, and it's making me feel so confused."[24] Harlequins build this tension and then relieve it with the fantasy that love will tame the brute: "'I never will frighten you again, my darling,' he promised, and she knew without any doubt at all that he spoke the truth."[25] Readers are drawn to this emotionally powerful combination of reality and fantasy.

Harlequins also speak to women's ambiguous feelings about sexuality. Women are simultaneously punished for being sexual and for not being sexual in our society. On the one hand, if they express their sexuality freely, they are labeled threatening or promiscuous. On the other hand, if they do not express their sexuality, they are deemed frigid. Harlequins portray heroines caught in both of these positions and women can sympathize with their dilemma.

The pressure on women to be sexual is a relatively new development. Earlier it was sufficient for women to merely endure sex out of marital duty; it was believed that women had no sexual nature. As sex researchers began to "discover" women's sexuality and their orgasmic capacity, expectations about women's sexuality rose. The effects of these new ideas were contradictory: some women were relieved that they no longer had to hide their sexual responses but others experienced this new approach to sexuality as just another demand placed on them to perform according to the expectations of others. After years of being taught that good girls should not like sex and that a man would not respect them if they "let" him have sex with them before marriage, suddenly they were being told that women should like sex and that if they did not sexually satisfy their man, he could always go somewhere else to "get it." Overcoming a lifetime of sexual repression is not easy but Harlequins reassure women that it is possible:

> In that one swift moment she told him all that he needed to know. The loneliness and the repression that had been her childhood had slipped away from her. She was completely confident that she could give him anything he wanted.[26]

Sex in Harlequins is magical; ecstasy is achieved with ease. Once again, we see the seductive combination of a realistic problem and a fantasy solution.

Women are drawn to Harlequins because these happy endings make them feel good. One reader describes this motive with considerable candor:

> I just think that little bit of feeling good makes you read a Harlequin. 'Cause you look at the news, there's nothing good on the news. They only give you news of a disaster ... or an earth-shattering thing. You look at your kids. They're dirty and grimy. You have to keep constantly ... doing your job for them and your husband ... and the whole

thing is so tedious that just this little bit that I guess you find in it ...
drives you back.

In her studies of romance readers, Janice Radway interviewed
women who openly compared their use of romances to the use of
tranquilizers:

> "Many of them that I talked to said, 'Well, you know, it's just like
> drinking or it's just like popping pills. Only this doesn't harm anybody.
> This doesn't hurt my family, and it really doesn't hurt me, either. But it
> makes me happy and hopeful."[27]

Harlequins thus appeal to readers because they set up stressful situations that affect women in real life and then they inevitably resolve
that conflict, distracting and comforting women in the process.

* * *

Understanding why women read romances, however, is only the first
step in understanding their social significance. We also need to know
how romances affect readers. Determining effect is not easy since
women, aware of the stigma of romances, may be guarded in their
replies to questions about effect or they may be unconscious of the
effect romances have on them. Nevertheless, I tried to probe for some
answers to this crucial question in my interviews with readers.

I did not find much evidence that women attempt to model themselves after Harlequin heroines. Nor did I find widespread support
for the notion that romances unrealistically shape women's expectations about relationships. The vast majority of readers – the casual
readers – keep their romances imaginatively separate from reality.
One woman who told me that she preferred reading Harlequins to
reading about World War II added: "Yet I know ... that's happened
and it's reality whereas this is not reality." Another reader echoed
her distinction: "I think of them [the characters in Harlequins] as
being cardboard or movie style, eh? And you know, you enjoy them
because they're that and because your life is different and because
you are different." Still others commented that romances are
"make-believe" or "adult fairy tales" that do not carry over into
reality. Keen readers like the Black woman who measured the men
she met by Harlequin hero standards and very young women may
have a difficult time distinguishing fiction from reality, but most
women do not.

Every question I asked about effect – would you like to be married to a Harlequin hero? Have Harlequins made any changes in your life? Have Harlequins made you more romantic or affected your attitudes about relationships in any way? – drew a negative response from the majority of readers. Harlequin Enterprises' consumer research also found negligible effect:

> Most readers, however, don't take their romances that seriously. When asked if the books affect their everyday lives, all of the women surveyed by Harlequin's public relations firm of Dorf/ MJH Inc. responded that romances have no influence beyond the prosaic: Readers said they sometimes spent too much time and money on the books.[28]

Resisting the Harlequin fantasy is not always easy for readers. One reader related her struggle to keep the romances in perspective:

> Yes, it does affect me.... Say I've just finished a book and you've got a good feeling.... You know, he [her husband] can wreck that high kind of quickly ... by not coming across the way I figured he should.... And then ... you realize what a dummy you were to let it go, to let it affect you.

This woman has learned to recognize and control the impact romances have on her, but others make no effort to resist. A few women told me that reading Harlequins made them wish they were involved with a man who was strong and "masterful." I discovered, however, that when these seemingly straightforward acknowledgments of the negative effect romances have on women were put into context, they lost some of their critical edge. For example, I talked to one young woman, a self-identified feminist, who admitted that she was attracted to the strong heroes in romantic fiction. She felt that her intelligence intimidated men and reflected: "I'd like to meet someone who is stronger than I am who I couldn't manipulate and control and I'd have to learn a different way ..." Her traditional fantasy of a strong man, which she borrowed from romances, exists alongside her desire for equality and personal growth. Such individual complexities made predicting or determining effect difficult. Readers do not come to romances *tabula rasa,* ready to be moulded according to Harlequin specifications. Each woman brings her own set of values to bear upon the romances that has an influence on what messages she receives and accepts.

One final factor that must be taken into consideration in the discussion of effect is opportunity. Women can only model themselves after Harlequin heroines and establish intense love relationships with heroes if they have the opportunity to do so, which they do not. There are simply no real opportunities for women to live like Harlequin heroines even if they wanted to – not for an elderly woman living in a senior high-rise, not for a busy housewife and mother who has to have the organizational abilities of a major general to plan a trip to the supermarket, not for American Black women who outnumber available Black men five to one, not for employed women who are surrounded by other women in much the same position as themselves. Critics who are afraid that readers will try to imitate Harlequins may have a harder time distinguishing between reality and fantasy than readers do!

* * *

Clearly, the old stereotypes do not come close to describing the range of women who read romances nor do they address the complex ways in which women read. Women value Harlequins for their formulaic structure, which allows them to read under difficult conditions and which provides them with easy education and entertainment. Furthermore, the romances appeal emotionally to readers by resolving some of the major problems that women face in our society. Readers are cheered by this optimism. Although a minority of women become destructively "addicted" to Harlequins, most women are casual readers who view romances as a momentary escape into an imaginative world separate from their own, not as a way of life to be desired and emulated.

*

CHAPTER EIGHT

HAPPILY EVER AFTER?

My intention has been to explain the appeal of Harlequin romances from the perspective of the millions of women who read them. Most people's perceptions of romances are biased by their reliance on mimetic fiction standards, the "double critical standard" and other preconceived judgments about what romances should or should not be and how readers are affected by them. I have argued that we must listen to readers' own explanations of why they like romances and find the connections between the structure of women's lives and the content of their fantasies before we can understand the significance of romantic fiction. When we do this, we discover that Harlequins speak to women about some of the problems they face in our society. Concern about economic security, loneliness, powerlessness and sexual violence against women pervades romances. After posing these threats, however, Harlequins reassure women with inevitably happy endings. In a romance, no problem is so great that it cannot be solved by a combination of individual initiative, fate and the power of love. Harlequins clearly meet readers' needs for excitement and security, one of the primary functions of formula fiction according to John Cawelti. Readers are attracted to not only the content of romances but to their format as well. Their predictability and uniformity are valued by women who want cheap, reliable, easy reading that they can pick up and put down at their convenience.

I have also argued that we must analyze the commercial system that produces romances to understand why we get the kinds and numbers of romances that we do. We have seen that Harlequin Enterprises, the leading publisher of romantic fiction, has done everything in its power to heighten the demand for romances. Its elaborate advertising campaigns, reader parties and give-away programs have increased the number of new readers and reinforced the loyalty of established ones. Yet, for all of its past impressive growth and profitability, Harlequin's power is limited by the increasing competition it faces in the romance industry and by the sometimes unpredictable demands of readers.

Leslie Fiedler has commented on publishers' scramble to determine what people want in their popular culture:

> Far from manipulating mass taste, its so-called masters breathlessly pursue it, cutting each other's throats, risking bankruptcy to find images which the great audience will recognize as dreams they have already dreamed, or would if they could. No wonder they think of themselves as riding a tiger ...[1]

At the beginning of the romance boom in the middle 1970s, Harlequin officials thought they had the tiger by the tail but they were mistaken. The sweet love stories that had been popular for a hundred years needed to be updated and brought into the twentieth century. The sales of a romance line began to reflect its success in satisfactorily adding a skillful blend of sexuality and realism to the traditional romance formula. Harlequin lagged behind other publishers in making these changes and their share of the market dropped as a result. Thus, as a corporate producer of romantic fiction, Harlequin Enterprises both controls and is controlled by women's desire for romances. The romances we get are a product of a literary history, contemporary social changes and the corporate drive for profitability.

We must continue to explore the complex relationship between the romance industry, romantic fiction and readers, with particular attention paid to readers. Most analysts still view romance readers as an undifferentiated mass although research indicates that there is a broad range in their characteristics. We need to further investigate the extent and significance of these differences. Although no specific age, marital status or economic group of women seems to be more attracted to romances than any other group, we cannot discount the possibility that they appeal to certain personality types. The psychology of romance readers needs to be studied in more depth and compared to that of other women readers who do not like romantic fiction. In conjunction with these efforts, we must also look at men readers and their fantasy literature. What do they read, why and how are they affected? Are there gender differences in men's and women's relationships to formula fiction – and if so, what are they?

Romantic fiction trends should continue to be scrutinized. The last few years have been a period of extensive experimentation and the future of the romance is unclear. As we've seen, romances are ambivalent and even contradictory about many aspects of women's lives, most notably their commitment to the labour force, their attitudes towards equality in heterosexual relationships and their response to sexual violence. Can these contradictions be worked out in the romances or will they persist? Will some of the positive trends that have emerged recently continue, or will the genre backtrack? How much realism can the romance formula accommodate before it is no longer a romance? What risks are publishers willing to take in an effort to expand their market? Although romance sales continue to rise, the number of books returned unsold to the publishers has also greatly increased. This indicates that the industry is overcrowded and business journals are predicting a "shakedown" in the near future. Who will survive?

As one of the oldest and largest romance publishers, Harlequin Enterprises' role in the industry will be interesting to watch. Will Harlequin live happily ever after? Predictions are risky and difficult to make, considering how quickly changes have occurred in the recent past. Although competition and variable quality have eroded readers' brand-name loyalty, Harlequin still has the advantage of being the "original" contemporary category romance series. In addition, it has the largest international distribution of all the romance publishers. The home market is nearly saturated, but Harlequin's sales abroad have steadily increased. (This international cultural penetration is another phenomenon worthy of study. What messages do readers in developing countries receive from North American romances? What impact do romances have on diverse national, racial and ethnic cultures?) Harlequin has added several new series of romances to accommodate readers' evolving tastes and it has expanded its operations to include male fantasy literature, a less developed field with potential for growth. I do not know if these advantages and adaptations will be sufficient to pull Harlequin out of its slump. Only one thing is certain: romances as a form of escape fiction have been popular for hundreds of years and they will survive the romance industry "shakedown" whether Harlequin Enterprises does or not!

*

NOTES

CHAPTER I NOTES

[1] Daisy Maryles and Robert Dahlin, "Romance Fiction," *Publishers Weekly*, Vol. 220 (November 13, 1981), p. 25; Rosemary Guiley, *Love Lines: The Romance Reader's Guide to Printed Pleasures* (Facts on File Publications, 1983), p. 2.

[2] Stephen Bronte, "Japan's Passion for Harlequin," *Financial Post*, March 22, 1980, p. 17; C. Sue Scully, "Harlequin Enterprises Ltd.," *Midland Doherty Limited*, May 1979.

[3] John Cawelti, *Adventure, Mystery, and Romance* (University of Chicago Press, 1976), p. 8.

[4] *Ibid.*, pp. 9-14.

[5] *Ibid.*, p. 13.

[6] *Ibid.*, p. 19.

[7] *Ibid.*, p. 16.

[8] Ian Watt, *The Rise of the Novel* (Penguin Books, 1957), p. 50.

[9] Leslie Fiedler, *Love and Death in the American Novel* (Stein and Day, 1966), p. 42.

[10] Watt, p. 154.

[11] Ann Douglas, *The Feminization of American Culture* (Avon Books, 1977), p. 72.

[12] Watt, pp. 55, 58.

[13] Elaine Showalter, *A Literature of Their Own: British Women Novelists From Bronte to Lessing* (Princeton University Press, 1977), pp. 79-80.

[14] Tania Modleski, *Loving With a Vengeance: Mass-Produced Fantasies For Women* (Archon Books, 1982), p. 11.

[15] Cawelti, pp. 41-42.

[16] Leslie Fiedler, *What Was Literature? Class Culture and Mass Society* (Simon and Schuster, 1982), p. 80; Maryles and Dahlin, *op. cit.*

[17] Elene Kolb, "The Great Escape – Male and Female," *Publishers Weekly*, Vol. 220 (November 13, 1981), p. 32.

[18] Modleski, p. 57.

[19] *Ibid.*, pp. 43, 50-51, 58.

[20] Mariam Darce Frenier, "Harlequins: The 'Traditional' Woman Takes On The Sexual Revolution" (Paper given at the Eleventh Annual Convention of the Popular Culture Association, March 25-29, 1981), pp. 1, 39-40.

[21] Janet Patterson, "Consuming Passion," *Fireweed*, 11 (1981), p. 20.

[22] Ann Snitow, "Mass Market Romance: Pornography for Women is Different," *Radical History Review*, 20 (Spring/Summer 1979), p. 143.

[23] Ann Douglas, "Soft-Porn Culture: Punishing the Liberated Woman," *The New Republic*, Vol. 183, No. 9 (August 30, 1980); Snitow, p. 156.

[24] Beatrice Faust, *Women, Sex, and Pornography* (Macmillan, 1980), pp. 18.

[25] Mary Burchell, *Yours with Love* (Harlequin Enterprises, 1981), pp. 74-74. (Subsequent references to Harlequin Enterprises will be indicated by H.E.)

[26] Daphne Clair, *The Loving Trap* (H.E., 1982), p.30.

[27] Essie Summers, *Through All the Years* (H.E., 1975), p. 146.

[28] Elizabeth Graham, *Stormy Vigil* (H.E., 1982), p. 42.

[29] *Ibid.*, p. 143.

CHAPTER 2 NOTES

[1] *Thirty Years of Harlequin 1949-1979* (H.E., 1979), pp. 18-33.

[2] Harlequin Enterprises Publicity Release, undated.

[3] Donald Redekop, "For this publisher, books are a product to be sold as if they were candy bars," *Financial Post*, August 9, 1975, p. C8.

[4] Sheri Craig, "Harlequin took a page from P&G s marketing book to sell 'romance,'" *Marketing*, October 13, 1975, p. 16.

[5] Barbara Rudolph, "Heartbreak comes to Harlequin," *Forbes,* March 29, 1982, p. 50.

[6] *Harlequin Enterprises Limited, Annual Report,* 1980, pp. 30-31; "Expanding Romance Market," *New York Times,* March 8, 1982, p. 24.

[7] Peggy Berkowitz, "Harlequin's Formula Romance Books Face Stiff Battle in Newly Competitive Industry," *Wall Street Journal,* July 21, 1983, p. 25.

[8] Halyna Perun, "Harlequin lays off 85 workers in bid to halt profits' plunge," *Globe and Mail,* September 17, 1983.

[9] Robert Fulford, "Notebook – Now if all the rest of you would just act like Harlequin books …," *Saturday Night* XCI (October 1976), p. 7.

[10] Phyllis Berman, "They Call Us Illegitimate," *Forbes,* March 6, 1978, p. 37.

[11] Craig, p. 14.

[12] John Cawelti, *Adventure, Mystery, and Romance* (University of Chicago Press, 1976), p. 34.

[13] Personal interview with Fred Kerner at Harlequin Enterprises in 1977.

[14] *Harlequin* (magazine produced by the company), V No. 9, p. 4.

[15] Stephen Bronte, "Japan's Passion for Harlequin," *Financial Post,* March 22, 1980, p. 17.

[16] Berman, p. 38.

[17] Redekop, *op. cit.*

[18] "Harlequin Launches Million-Dollar TV Campaign in U.S. Market," *Publishers Weekly,* CCVIII (September 29, 1975), p. 38.

[19] Mary Novik, "A Harlequin Serenade," *Books in Canada,* Vol. 7, No. 9 (November 1978), p. 4.

[20] Harlequin Enterprises Publicity Release, undated.

[21] Jack Willoughby, "Harlequin's chief's projections show more happy endings on movie screen," *Globe and Mail,* July 16, 1977, p. B5.

[22] Redekop, *op. cit.*

[23] Advertisement, *Ladies Home Journal* XCIV (July 1977), p. 10.

[24] Alice K. Turner, "The Romance of Harlequin Enterprises," *Publishers Weekly* CCIV (September 3, 1973), p. 31.

[25] See *Good Housekeeping,* April 1976; Claire Gerus, "Love for Sale," *Financial Post Magazine,* February 10, 1979, p. 44.

[26] "Harlequin Launches Million-Dollar TV Campaign," *op. cit.*

[27] Turner, p. 31.

[28] Craig, p. 14.

[29] Advertisement, Compton Advertising Inc., *Book Trade,* Facsimile, Harlequin Enterprises Publicity Release, undated.

[30] Willoughby, *op. cit.*

[31] Ontario Public Interest Research Group, *Reed International: profile of a transnational corporation* OPIRG Inc., 1977), p. 1.

[32] *Harlequin Enterprises Limited, Annual Report,* 1979, p. 19.

[33] *Ibid.*

[34] Miles Kimball catalogue, Vol. 2A 1982, p. 3.

[35] *Harlequin Enterprises Limited, Annual Report,* 1980, p. 4.

[36] David Weinberger, "The case of yellow fever," *Macleans* Vol. 94 (September 14, 1981), p. 72.

[37] Mack Bolan, *Return to Vietnam* (Worldwide, 1982), p. 56.

[38] *Ibid.,* p. 22.

[39] *Ibid.,* p. 88-89.

[40] Willoughby, *op. cit.*

[41] Sid Adilman, "Harlequin gives U.S. firm an option for 12 TV films," *Toronto Star,* October 12, 1983.

[42] The Financial Post 500, *Financial Post,* June 1982, pp. 74-75.

[43] Bronte, *ibid.*

[44] C. Sue Scully, "Harlequin Enterprises Ltd.," *Midland Doherty Limited,* May 1979.

[45] *Moody's Industrial Manual* (Moody's Investors Service, Inc., 1981), Vol. I p. 1333.

[46] "Harlequin: A romance publisher adds men's novels and a touch of mystery," *Business Week,* July 6, 1981, p. 94.

[47] Dorothy Smith, "An Analysis of Ideological Structures and How Women Are Excluded," *Canadian Review of Sociology and Anthropology* XII (November 1975), p. 357.

[48] *Ibid.,* pp. 354-55.

[49] In the *Financial Post Corporation Service* card on Torstar, all male members of the board are listed by their first and middle initials and last names, in contrast with the women members, whose first names are written out – Ruth Hindmarsh and Catherine Crang. The women are, therefore, clearly identified and identifiable.

[50] Smith, p. 362.

[51] *Ibid.*, p. 364.

[52] Jane Davidson, "Analysts differ on Torstar's prospects if firm acquires rest of Harlequin shares," *Globe and Mail,* December 30, 1980, p. B8.

[53] *Ibid.*

[54] *Ibid.*

[55] Rudolph, p. 50.

[56] Davidson, *op. cit.*

[57] "Torstar Corporation," *Financial Post Corporation Service,* May 31, 1982.

CHAPTER 3 NOTES

[1] "Virgin territory," *Forbes,* June 23, 1980, p. 17.

[2] "Harlequin: A romance publisher adds men's novels and a touch of mystery," *Business Week,* July 6, 1981, p. 94. My emphasis.

[3] N.R. Kleinfield, "Publishers Find Romances Pay," *New York Times,* May 25, 1978, p. D1.

[4] J.D. Reed, "From Bedroom to Boardroom," *Time,* April, 13, 1981, p. 101.

[5] Rosemary Guiley, *Love Lines: The Romance Reader's Guide to Printed Pleasures* (Facts on File Publications, 1983), p. 2.

[6] Daisy Maryles, "Some Facts and Figures," *Publishers Weekly* Vol. 220 (November 13, 1981), p. 26.

[7] "Why Book Publishers Are No Longer In Love With Romance Novels," *Business Week,* December 5, 1983, p. 157.

[8] Diane Wilson, "Passion! Fury! The battle for the romance novel market," *Canadian Business,* July 1980, p. 24.

[9] Elene M. Kolb, "Checking Out the Categories," *Publishers Weekly, op. cit.*, p. 46.

[10] Beatrice W. Small, "What is Romance Fiction?" *Publishers Weekly, op. cit.*, p. 28.

[11] Stephen Cook, "Romance Industry News," *Romantic Times,* Fall, No. 7, 1982, p. 21.

[12] Wendy Smith, "An Earlier Start on Romance," *Publishers Weekly, op. cit.*, p. 56.

[13] *Ibid.*, p. 58.

[14] Barbara Cartland, *Vote for Love* (Bantam Books, 1977), p. 150.

[15] Alice Morgan, *The Sands of Malibu* (Dell, 1982), p. 93.

[16] Kolb, *op. cit.*

[17] Elene M. Kolb, "The Books You Judge By Their Covers," *Publishers Weekly, op. cit.*, p. 42.

[18] *Ibid.*, p. 44.

[19] Barbara Rudolph, "Heartbreak comes to Harlequin," *Forbes,* March 29, 1982, p. 50.

[20] Peggy Berkowitz, "Harlequin's Formula Romance Books Face Stiff Battle in Newly Competitive Industry," *Wall Street Journal,* July 21, 1983, p. 25.

[21] Stephen Cook, "Romance Industry News," *Romantic Times,* Summer No. 6, 1982, p. 20.

[22] Rudolph, p. 51.

[23] *Ibid.*, p. 50.

[24] Reed, *op. cit.*

[25] Stella Dong, "Selling Romances: Often Right Out of the Boxes," *Publishers Weekly, op. cit.*, p. 61.

[26] *Ibid.*, p. 62.

[27] Rudolph, *op. cit.*

[28] "Scaling The Heights," *Brooklyn Heights Press,* January 14, 1982.

[29] Rudolph, *op. cit.*

[30] "News Flash!" *Romantic Times,* Fall No. 7, 1982, p. 9.

[31] Jamie Raab, "Romance On the Job," *Romantic Times,* Summer No. 6 1982, p. 21.

[32] Elizabeth Hoy, "Elizabeth Hoy," *Thirty Years Of Harlequin* (H.E, 1979), p. 205. Subsequent references to the autobiographies in this work will refer to the book as *Harlequin*.

[33] Nina Baym, *Woman's Fiction: A Guide to Novels by and about Women in America, 1820-1870* (Cornell University Press, 1978), p. 30.

[34] Kathryn Falk, *Love's Leading Ladies* (Pinnacle Books, 1982), p. 63.

[35] Reed, *op. cit.*

[36] *Ibid.*

[37] Kathryn Falk, "Are Romance Writers' Associations Necessary?" *Romantic Times,* Summer No. 6, 1982, p. 27.

[38] Doris E. Smith, "Doris E. Smith," *Harlequin,* p. 231.

[39] Lilian Peake, "Lilian Peake," *ibid.*, p. 225.

[40] Mary Wibberley, "Mary Wibberley," *ibid.*, pp. 247-48.

[41] Yvonne Whittal, "Yvonne Whittal," *ibid.*, p. 246.

[42] Helen Bianchin, "Helen Bianchin," *ibid.*, p. 168.

[43] Janet Dailey, "Janet Dailey," *ibid.*, p. 177.

[44] Richard Hoggart, *The Uses of Literacy* (Penguin Books, 1957), p. 209.

[45] Falk, *Love's Leading Ladies, op. cit.*, p. 42.

[46] *Ibid.*, p. 337.

CHAPTER 4 NOTES

[1] Sue Peters, *Clouded Waters* (H. E., 1976).

[2] Stella Francis Nel, *Golden Harvest* (H.E., 1973), p. 187.

[3] Margaret Malcolm, *Little Savage* (H.E., 1968), p. 4.

[4] Elizabeth Hoy, *Into a Golden Land* (H.E., 1971), pp. 64, 187.

[5] Violet Winspear, *The Man She Married* (H.E., 1983), p. 122.

[6] Charlotte Lamb, *Desire* (H.E., 1981), p. 77.

[7] Frank Parkin, *Class Inequality and Political Order* (Paladin, 1971), p. 77.

[8] Anne Hampson, *The Rebel Bride* (H.E., 1973), p. 25.

[9] *Harlequin*, v (No. 8), p. 5.

[10] Rosalind Brett, *Sweet Waters* (H.E., 1964), p. 93.

[11] Violet Winspear, *Desert Doctor* (H.E., 1965), pp. 5-6; Nel, p. 16; Brett, p. 103.

[12] Rosalind Brett, *Young Tracy* (H.E., 1964), p. 168.

[13] *Harlequin*, IV (No. 7), p. 4.

[14] *Harlequin*, IV (No. 5), p. 5; *Harlequin*, IV (No. 9), p. 5.

[15] Leslie Fiedler, *Love and Death in the American Novel* (Stein and Day, 1966), p. 163.

[16] Marjorie Norrell, *Promise the Doctor* (H.E., 1966), p. 191.

[17] Jayne Bavling, *Wait for the Storm* (H.E., 1982), p. 165.

[18] Margaret Dalziel, *Popular Fiction 100 Years Ago* (Cohen and West, 1957), pp. 97-98.

[19] See respectively, Joanna Russ, "Somebody's Trying to Kill Me and I Think It's My Husband: The Modern Gothic," *Journal of Popular Culture,* VI

(Spring 1973), pp. 666-91; Philippe Perebinossoff, "What Does a Kiss Mean? The Love Comic Formula and the Creation of the Ideal Teenage Girl," *Journal of Popular Culture*, VIII (Spring 1975), pp. 825-35; Lovelle Ray, "The American Woman in Mass Media: How Much Emancipation and What does It Mean?" in Constantina Safiolios-Rothschild, ed., *Toward a Sociology of Women* (Xerox College Publishing, 1972), pp. 41-62; David Sonenschein, "Love and Sex in the Romance Magazines," in George Lewis, ed., *Side-Saddle on the Golden Calf* (Goodyear Publishing, 1972), pp. 66-74.

[20] Sonenschein, p. 70.

[21] John Cawelti, *Adventure, Mystery, and Romance* (University of Chicago Press, 1976), p. 18.

[22] Cawelti, p. 6.

[23] Deborah David and Robert Brannon, *The Forty-Nine Percent Majority* (Addison-Wesley, 1976), p. 12.

[24] Kay Mussell, "Beautiful and Damned: The Sexual Woman in Gothic Fiction," *Journal of Popular Culture*, IX (Summer 1975), pp. 84-89.

[25] Elizabeth Hunter, *Spiced With Cloves* (H.E., 1966), p. 71.

[26] Russ, *ibid.*

CHAPTER 5 NOTES

[1] Carl N. Degler, *At Odds: Women and the Family in America from the Revolution to the Present* (Oxford University Press, 1980), pp. 131-32, 418.

[2] The Women's Bureau, Ontario Ministry of Labour, *Women in the Labour Force "Basic Facts"* (Ontario Ministry of Labour, Women's Bureau, undated), pp. 1-3; Council on the Economic Status of Women, St. Paul, Minnesota, Newsletter No.59 (March 1982), p. 30.

[3] The Women's Bureau, p. 4.

[4] Council on the Economic Status of Women, p. 3.

[5] *Ibid.*, p. 4.

[6] Jane Donnelly, *Rocks Under Shining Water* (H.E., 1973), p. 71; Joyce Dingwell, *Corporation Boss* (H.E., 1976), p. 56.

[7] Sara Seale, *Cloud Castle* (H.E., 1967), p. 176.

[8] Sarah Holland, *The Devil's Mistress* (H.E., 1982), p. 175.

[9] Patricia Lake, *The Silver Casket* (H.E., 1983), p. 55.

[10] Nerina Hilliard, *Dark Star* (H.E., 1969), pp. 15, 119.

[11] Lucy Gillen, *The Pretty Witch* (H.E., 1974), p. 14.

[12] Marlene Kadar, "Sexual Harassment as a Form of Social Control," in *Still Ain't Satisfied*, eds. Maureen FitzGerald, Connie Guberman and Margie Wolfe (Women's Press, 1982), p. 171.

[13] Nicola West, *Lucifer's Brand* (H.E., 1983), pp. 46-47.

[14] *Ibid.*, pp. 58-59.

[15] *Ibid.*, p. 81.

[16] Sally Wentworth, *Flying High* (H.E., 1983), p. 79.

[17] Gillen, p. 180.

[18] Kay Thorpe, *Rising Star* (H.E., 1969), p. 190.

[19] West, p. 121.

[20] Mary Wibberley, *Dark Viking* (H.E., 1975), p. 66.

[21] Flora Kidd, *Between Pride and Passion* (H.E., 1982), pp. 95, 142-43.

[22] *Ibid.*, p. 166.

[23] Sally Wentworth, *Liberated Lady* (H.E., 1979), p. 17.

[24] *Ibid.*, pp. 163-64.

[25] M. Patricia Connelly, "Women as Reserve Labour: The Canadian Case" (Paper given at the Canadian Sociology and Anthropology Association Meetings, June 1977), p. 12.

[26] Dingwell, p. 74.

[27] Elizabeth Hunter, *Spiced With Cloves* (H.E., 1966), p. 16.

[28] Essie Summers, *Through All The Years* (H.E., 1975), p. 66.

[29] Ann Oakley, *The Sociology of Housework* (Pantheon Books, 1974), pp. 55, 57.

[30] Summers, p. 54.

[31] Lake, p. 189.

[32] *Harlequin*, IV (No. 5), p. 4.

[33] *Harlequin*, IV (No. 8), p. 7.

[34] Ann Weale, *Islands of Summer* (H.E., 1965), p. 26.

[35] Jayne Bavling, *Wait for the Storm* (H.E., 1982), p. 110.

[36] Kay Deaux, *The Behavior of Women and Men* (Brooks/Cole Publishing Co., 1976), pp. 87-88, 71, 123.

[37] Jean Mayer, *Overweight: Causes, Cost, and Control* (Prentice-Hall, 1968), p. 91; Marcia Millman, *Such a Pretty Face* (W.W. Norton and Co., 1980), pp. 90-94.

[38] Jan Andersen, *Master of Koros* (H.E., 1974), p. 110.

[39] Alexandra Sellers, *Season of Storm* (H.E., 1983), p. 178.

[40] Dorothy Cork, *A Promise to Keep* (H.E., 1974), p. 103.

[41] Wentworth, *Liberated Lady,* p. 121.

[42] Sandra Field, *The Winds of Winter* (H.E., 1981), p. 121.

[43] Ian Robertson, *Sociology* (Worth Publishers, 1977), p. 329.

[44] Dair Gillespie, "Who Has the Power? The Marital Struggle," in *Family, Marriage and the Struggle of the Sexes,* ed. Hans Peter Dreitzel (Macmillan, 1972), pp. 128-46.

[45] Roumelia Lane, *Harbour of Deceit* (H.E., 1975), p. 188.

[46] Dingwell, p. 187.

[47] Ann Weale, *A Touch of the Devil* (H.E., 1982), p. 21.

[48] Elizabeth Graham, *Stormy Vigil* (H.E., 1982), p. 188.

[49] Judith Long Laws and Pepper Schwartz, *Sexual Scripts: The Social Construction of Female Sexuality* (Dryden Press, 1977), p. 51.

[50] Charlotte Lamb, *Desire* (H.E., 1981), p. 120.

[51] Yvonne Whittal, *Chains of Gold* (H.E., 1983), p. 102.

[52] Amanda Doyle, *Play The Tune Softly* (H.E., 1967), p. 187.

[53] Sara Craven, *Dark Summer Dawn* (H.E., 1982), p. 93.

[54] Joyce Dingwell, *Greenfingers Farm* (H.E., 1966), pp. 56-57.

[55] Long Laws and Schwartz, p. 113.

[56] Kay Thorpe, *Temporary Marriage* (H.E., 1982), p. 71.

[57] Wentworth, *Flying High,* p. 107.

[58] Penny Jordan, *Marriage Without Love* (H.E., 1981), p. 123.

[59] Yvonne Whittal, *The Lion of LaRoche* (H.E., 1982), pp. 107-108.

[60] Anne Hampson, *The Rebel Bride* (H.E., 1973), p. 171.

[61] Esther Wyndham, *Once You Have Found Him* (H.E., 1964), p. 184.

[62] Whittal, *The Lion of LaRoche,* p. 108.

[63] Holland, p. 186.

[64] Margaret Pargeter, *Not Far Enough* (H.E., 1982), p. 51.

[65] Rosemary Carter, *Daredevil* (H.E., 1983), p. 42.

[66] Anne Hampson, *South of the Moon* (H.E., 1979), p. 108.

[67] Anne Hampson, *For Love of a Pagan* (H.E., 1979), p. 102.

[68] Joanna Russ, "Somebody's Trying to Kill Me and I Think It's My Husband," *Journal of Popular Culture,* Vol. 6, No. 4 (Spring 1973), pp. 666-91.

[69] Anne Hampson, *To Tame a Vixen* (H.E., 1979), p. 32.

[70] Sally Wentworth, *The Judas Kiss* (H.E., 1982), p. 165.

[71] Holland, p. 37.

[72] Mary Burchell, *Yours With Love* (H.E., 1981), p. 182.

[73] Thorpe, pp. 45-46.

CHAPTER 6 NOTES

[1] Carole Mortimer, *Perfect Partner* (H.E., 1983), p. 31.

[2] Charlotte Lamb, *Midnight Lover* (H.E., 1982), p. 8.

[3] Violet Winspear, *The Man She Married* (H.E., 1983), p. 155.

[4] Mortimer, p. 84.

[5] Carole Mortimer, *Red Rose for Love* (H.E., 1982), p. 70.

[6] Patricia Lake, *The Silver Casket* (H.E., 1983), p. 22; Elizabeth Ashton, *My Lady Disdain* (H.E., 1976), p. 86.

[7] Sara Craven, *Dark Summer Dawn* (H.E., 1982), p. 9; Sandra Field, *Walk By My Side* (H.E., 1983), p. 40.

[8] Jayne Bavling, *Wait for the Storm* (H.E., 1982), p. 10; Elizabeth Graham, *Stormy Vigil* (H.E., 1982), p. 5; Sally Wentworth, *Flying High* (H.E., 1983), p. 17.

[9] Kay Clifford, *No Time For Love* (H.E., 1982), p. 45.

[10] Charlotte Lamb, *Desire* (H.E., 1981), pp. 35-36.

[11] Marjorie Lewty, *The Short Engagement* (H.E., 1978), p. 123.

[12] Margaret Way, *Broken Rhapsody* (H.E., 1982), p. 23.

[13] Janine Ellis, *Rough Justice* (H.E., 1980), p. 39.

[14] Charlotte Lamb, *Midnight Lover,* p. 135.

[15] Sally Wentworth, *Liberated Lady* (H.E., 1979), pp. 98-99.

[16] Margaret Benston, "The Political Economy of Women's Liberation," in *Woman in a Man-Made World,* eds. Nona Glazer and Helen Youngelson Waehrer (Rand McNally Publishing, 1977), pp. 216-25.

[17] Adrienne Rich, "Compulsory Heterosexuality and Lesbian Existence," in *Powers of Desire: The Politics of Sexuality,* eds. Ann Snitow, Christine Stancell, Sharon Thompson (New York: Monthly Review Press, 1983), pp. 177-205.

[18] Way, p. 77.

[19] Sheila Douglas, *Return to Lanmore* (H.E., 1980), p. 8.

[20] Linda Harrel, *Sea Lightning* (H.E., 1980), p. 15.

[21] Wentworth, *Flying High,* p.15.

[22] Mortimer, *Red Rose,* p. 28.

[23] Douglas, p. 76.

[24] Mortimer, *Perfect Partner,* p. 37.

[25] L.A. Peplau, Z. Rubin and C.T. Hill, "Sexual intimacy in dating relationships," *Journal of Social Issues,* 1977, 33 (2) pp. 86-109, cited in Susan Basow, *Sex-Role Stereotypes: Traditions and Alternatives* (Brooks/Cole Publishing, 1980), p. 219.

[26] Anne Hampson, *For Love of a Pagan* (H.E., 1979), pp. 139-140.

[27] Lewty, p. 129.

[28] Anne Weale, *A Touch of the Devil* (H.E., 1982), p. 95.

[29] Hilda Nickson, *The Sweet Spring* (H.E., 1972), p. 13.

[30] Hilda Pressley, *The Man in Possession* (H.E., 1970), p. 78.

[31] Lamb, *Desire,* p. 187.

[32] Penny Jordan, *Marriage Without Love* (H.E., 1982), p. 118.

[33] Harrel, p. 190.

[34] Martha Nelson, "Sweet Bondage: You and Your Romance Habit," *Ms,* Vol. xi No. 8 (February 1983), p. 97.

[35] Mariam Darce Frenier, "Harlequins: The 'Traditional' Woman Takes on The Sexual Revolution" (Paper delivered at the Eleventh Annual Convention of the Popular Culture Association, March 25-29, 1981.)

[36] Weale, pp. 31, 43.

[37] Clifford, p. 28.

[38] Dair Gillespie, "Who Has the Power? The Marital Struggle," in *Family, Marriage and the Struggle of the Sexes,* ed. Hans Peter Dreitzel (Macmillan, 1972), p. 140.

[39] Peter Blaw, *Exchange and Power in Social Life* (Wiley, 1964), pp. 78-80.

[40] Yvonne Whittal, *The Lion of LaRoche* (H.E., 1981), p. 181.

[41] Tania Modleski, *Loving With a Vengeance: Mass-Produced Fantasies for Women* (Archon Books, 1982), p. 45.

[42] Margaret Pargeter, *Not Far Enough* (H.E., 1982), p. 187.

[43] Jan Maclean, *An Island Loving* (H.E., 1982), p. 99.

[44] Winspear, p. 131.

[45] Katrina Britt, *Flowers for my Love* (H.E., 1980), p. 115.

[46] Graham, p. 163.

[47] Weale, p. 62.

[48] *Ibid.*, p. 104.

[49] Flora Kidd, *Passionate Stranger* (H.E., 1981), p. 186.

[50] Jane Corrie, *Rimmer's Way* (H.E., 1977), p. 188.

[51] Maclean, pp. 53-54; Field, p. 36; Graham, p. 36.

[52] Wentworth, *Liberated Lady,* pp. 25-26.

[53] Herb Goldberg, *The New Male* (Signet, 1979), p. 12.

[54] Graham, p. 6.

[55] Harrel, p. 189.

[56] Rosalie Henaghan, *Coppers Girl* (H.E., 1982), p. 115.

[57] Daphne Clair, *The Loving Trap* (H.E., 1982), p. 169.

[58] *Ibid.*, p. 176.

[59] *Ibid.*, p. 183.

[60] *Ibid.*, p. 184.

[61] William French, "Reality invades romance fiction," *Globe and Mail,* September 20, 1983.

[62] Mary Burchell, *Yours With Love* (H.E., 1981), p. 186.

CHAPTER 7 NOTES

[1] Peter Mann, *A New Survey: The Facts About Romantic Fiction* (Mills and Boon, 1974), p. 6.

[2] *Ibid.*, pp. 8-10.

[3] Kathryn Falk, "Who Reads Romances – And Why?" *Publishers Weekly,* Vol. 220 (November 13, 1981), p. 32.

[4] Carol Thurston, "The Liberation of Pulp Romances," *Psychology Today* (April 1983), p. 14.

[5] *Ibid.*

[6] Most of the interviews were done in 1977 in Hamilton, Ontario, while the remainder took place in Iowa and Minnesota in 1982-1983. Three techniques were used to obtain readers. I contacted fifteen readers through a used bookstore; these readers referred me to an additional nine. The remaining readers were referred to me through friends, family, students and colleagues.

[7] "Buying Harlequin Books Has Become a Habit, Like Buying Soap," *Progressive Grocer* (March 1976).

[8] Rosemary Guiley, *Love Lines: The Romance Reader's Guide to Printed Pleasures* (Facts on File Publications, 1983), p. 5. My emphasis.

[9] Falk, *op. cit.*

[10] *Harlequin,* VI (No. 6), p. 6.

[11] *Harlequin* (November 1978), p. 5.

[12] *Harlequin,* VI (No. 3), p. 4.

[13] Dorothy Richardson, "The Long Day, The Story of a New York Working Girl," in *Women at Work,* ed. William L. O'Neill (Quadrangle Books, 1972), p. 72.

[14] Erving Goffman, *Asylums* (Anchor Books, 1961), pp. 68-69.

[15] Ann Oakley, *The Sociology of Housework* (Pantheon Books, 1974), p. 85.

[16] *Harlequin,* III (No. 10), p. 4.

[17] Vermont Royster, "The Reading Addiction," *The Wall Street Journal* (June 24, 1981), p. 20.

[18] Tania Modleski, *Loving With a Vengeance* (Archon Books, 1982), p. 38.

[19] Janet Patterson, "Consuming Passion," *Fireweed,* Issue 11 (1981), p. 22.

[20] Susan A. Basow, *Sex-Role Stereotypes: Traditions and Alternatives* (Brooks/Cole Publishing, 1980), p. 259.

[21] See Martha Baum, "Love, Marriage, and the Division of Labor," and Dair Gillespie, "Who Has the Power? The Marital Struggle" in *Family, Marriage and the Struggle of the Sexes,* ed. Hans Peter Dreitzel (Macmillan, 1972).

[22] Jack O. Balswick and Charles W. Peek, "The Inexpressive Male: A Tragedy of American Society," in *The Forty-Nine Percent Majority,* eds. Deborah S. David and Robert Brannon (Addison-Wesley, 1976).

[23] "The Fear That Binds Us," Iris Video, Minneapolis-St. Paul, Minnesota, 1981.

[24] Rosemary Carter, *Daredevil* (H.E., 1983), p. 42.

[25] Anne Hampson, *For Love of a Pagan* (H.E., 1979), p. 186.

[26] Elizabeth Hunter, *Spiced With Cloves* (H.E., 1966), p. 192.

[27] Stanley Meisler, "Love in the fast racks," *Hamilton Spectator,* January 13, 1981, p. 37.

[28] George Paul Csicsery, "Splendor in the Cash," *Savvy* (December 1982), p. 60.

CHAPTER 8 NOTES

[1] Leslie Fiedler, *What Was Literature? Class Culture and Mass Society* (Simon and Schuster, 1982), p. 101.

BIBLIOGRAPHY

Adilman, Sid. "Harlequin gives u.s. firm an option for 12 TV films," *Toronto Star,* October 12, 1983.

Adorno, Theodor W. "Television and the Patterns of Mass Culture," *Mass Culture,* eds. Bernard Rosenberg and David Manning White. New York: The Free Press, 1957.

Andrews, Terry. "Romance in the Northland," *Mpls. St. Paul Magazine,* November 1981, pp. 127-30.

Armstrong, Pat and Hugh Armstrong. *The Double Ghetto: Canadian Women and their Segregated Work.* Toronto: McClelland and Stewart, 1978.

Baker Miller, Jean. *Toward a New Psychology of Women.* Boston: Beacon Press, 1976.

Balswick, Jack O. and Charles W. Peek. "The Inexpressive Male: A Tragedy of American Society," *The Forty-Nine Percent Majority: The Male Sex Role,* eds. Deborah S. David and Robert Brannon. Reading, Massachusetts: Addison-Wesley, 1976.

Basow, Susan A. *Sex-Role Stereotypes: Traditions and Alternatives.* Monterey, California: Brooks/Cole Publishing, 1980.

Baum, Martha. "Love, Marriage and the Division of Labor," *Family, Marriage and the Struggle of the Sexes,* ed. Hans Peter Dreitzel. New York: Macmillan, 1972.

Baym, Nina. *Woman's Fiction: A Guide to Novels by and about Women in America, 1820-1870.* Ithaca, New York: Cornell University Press, 1978.

Berkowitz, Peggy. "Harlequin's Formula Romance Books Face Stiff Battle in Newly Competitive Industry," *Wall Street Journal,* July 21, 1983, pp. 25, 35.

Berman, Phyllis. "They Call Us Illegitimate," *Forbes,* March 6, 1978, pp. 37-38.

Bronte, Stephen. "Japan's Passion for Harlequin," *Financial Post,* March 22, 1980, p. 17.

Brooklyn Press. "Scaling the Heights," January 14, 1982.

Business Week. "Why Book Publishers Are No Longer In Love With Romance Novels," December 5, 1983, pp. 157, 160.

— "Harlequin: A romance publisher adds men's novels and a touch of mystery," July 6, 1981, pp. 93-94.

Cartland, Barbara. "A Message from Barbara Cartland to the Romantic Book Lovers' Conference." Paper given at the Romantic Book Lovers' Conference, New York, New York, April 1982.

— *Vote for Love.* New York: Bantam Books, 1977.

Cawelti, John G. *Adventure, Mystery, and Romance.* Chicago: University of Chicago Press, 1976.

Connelly, M. Patricia. "Women as Reserve Labour: The Canadian Case." Paper given at the Canadian Sociology and Anthropology Association Meetings, June 1977.

Cook, Stephen. "Romance Industry News," *Romantic Times* 6 (Summer 1982), p. 20.

— "Romance Industry News," *Romantic Times* 7 (Fall 1982), p. 21.

Council on the Economic Status of Women. Newsletter No. 59. St. Paul, Minnesota, March 1982.

Craig, Sheri. "Harlequin Took a Page from P & G's Marketing Book to Sell 'Romance'," *Marketing,* October 13, 1975, pp. 14-16.

Csicsery, George Paul. "Splendor in the Cash," *Savvy,* December, 1982, pp. 58-60, 65, 67.

Dailey, Janet. "An Author's Own Story," *Harlequin* IV No. 8, pp. 62-63, 65.

Dalziel, Margaret. *Popular Fiction 100 Years Ago.* London: Cohen and West, 1957.

David, Deborah S. and Robert Brannon. *The Forty-Nine Percent Majority: The Male Sex Role.* Reading, Massachusetts: Addison-Wesley, 1976.

Davidson, Jane. "Analysts differ on Torstar's prospects if firm acquires rest of Harlequin shares," *Globe and Mail,* December 30, 1980, p. B8.

Deaux, Kay. *The Behavior of Women and Men.* Monterey, California: Brooks/Cole Publishing Company, 1976.

Degler, Carl N. *At Odds: Women and the Family in America from the Revolution to the Present.* New York: Oxford University Press, 1980.

Denato, Pat. "Romance novelists: The writers of the purple page," *Des Moines Register,* February 14, 1982, pp. 1, 6 E.

Dong, Stella. "Selling Romances: Often Right Out of the Boxes," *Publishers Weekly* 220 (November 13, 1981), pp. 61-63.

Douglas, Ann. *The Feminization of American Culture.* New York: Avon Books, 1977.

— "Soft-Porn Culture: Punishing the Liberated Woman," *The New Republic* Vol. 183, No. 9 (August 30, 1980), pp. 25-29.

Dowling, Colette. *The Cinderella Complex: Women's Hidden Fear of Independence.* New York: Pocket Books, 1981.

Falk, Kathryn, "Are Romance Writers' Associations Necessary?" *Romantic Times* 6 (Summer 1982), p. 27.

— *Love's Leading Ladies.* New York: Pinnacle Books, 1982.

— "Who Reads Romances – And Why," *Publishers Weekly* 220 (November 13, 1981), pp. 29, 32, 34.

Faust, Beatrice. *Women, Sex and Pornography: A Controversial Study.* New York: Macmillan, 1980.

Fiedler, Leslie. *Love and Death in the American Novel,* rev. ed. New York: Stein and Day, 1966.

— *What Was Literature? Class and Culture and Mass Society.* New York: Simon and Schuster, 1982.

Field, Sandra. "An Author's Own Story," *Harlequin* IV No. 4, pp. 66-68.

Forbes. "Virgin Territory," June 23, 1980, p. 17.

Fraser, Brian M. "Why Harlequin Enterprises Fell Out of Love with Science Fiction," *Financial Post,* December 17, 1977, pp. 16-18.

French, William. "Reality Invades Romance Fiction," *Globe and Mail,* September 20, 1983.

Frenier, Mariam Darce. "Harlequins: The 'Traditional' Woman Takes On The Sexual Revolution." Paper presented at the Eleventh Annual Convention of the Popular Culture Association, March 1981.

Fulford, Robert. "Now if All the Rest of You Would Just Act Like Harlequin Books," *Saturday Night* ICI (October 1976), pp. 6-9.

Gadbois, Sally. "The Great American Romance Novel," *Minneapolis Sun Weekender,* November 12, 1981, p. 7.

Gerus, Claire. "Love for Sale," *Financial Post Magazine,* February 10, 1979, pp. 42-44, 50, 52, 54.

Gillespie, Dair L. "Who Has the Power? The Marital Struggle," *Family, Marriage and the Struggle of the Sexes,* ed. Hans Peter Dreitzel. New York: Macmillan, 1972.

Goffman, Erving. *Asylums.* New York: Anchor Books, 1961.

Goldberg, Herb. *The Hazards of Being Male.* New York: Signet, 1976.

— *The New Male.* New York: Signet, 1979.

Guiley, Rosemary. *Love Lines: The Romance Reader's Guide to Printed Pleasures.* New York: Facts on File Publications, 1983.

Guthrie, R. Claire. "Sexual Harassment and Preventative Planning," *Lex Collegii* 5, No. 2 (Fall 1981), pp. 1-5.

Harlequin Books. *Thirty Years of Harlequin 1949-1979.* Toronto, 1979.

Haskell, Molly. "The 2,000-Year-Old Misunderstanding – 'Rape Fantasy,'" *Ms* v (November 1976), pp. 84-86, 92, 94, 96, 98.

Hazen, Helen. *Endless Rapture: Rape, Romance and the Female Imagination.* New York: Charles Scribner's Sons, 1983.

Hoggart, Richard. *The Uses of Literacy.* Harmondsworth, Middlesex, England: Penguin Books, 1957.

Horner, Matina J. "The measurement and behavioral implications of fear of success in women," *Personality, Motivation and Achievement,* eds. J.W. Atkinson and J.O. Raynor. Hemisphere, 1978.

Kadar, Marlene. "Sexual Harassment as a Form of Social Control," *Still Ain't Satisfied,* eds. Maureen FitzGerald, Connie Guberman and Margie Wolfe. Toronto: Women's Press, 1982.

Kephart, William M. "Some Correlates of Romantic Love," *Journal of Marriage and the Family* 29, No, 3 (August 1967), pp. 470-74.

Kleinfield, N.R. "Publishers Find Romances Pay," *New York Times,* May 25, 1978, pp. D1, D17.

Kolb, Elene M. "The Books You Judge By Their Covers," *Publishers Weekly* 220 (November 13, 1981), pp. 42, 44, 51.

— "Checking Out The Categories," *Publishers Weekly* 220 (November 13, 1981), p. 46.

— "The Great Escape – Male and Female," *Publishers Weekly* 220 (November 13, 1981), p. 32.

Kulik, J.A. and J. Harackiewicz. "Opposite-sex interpersonal attraction as a function of the sex roles of the perceiver and the perceived," *Sex Roles* 5 (1979), pp. 443-52.

Laws, Judith Long and Pepper Schwartz. *Sexual Scripts: The Social Construction of Female Sexuality*. Hinsdale, Illinois: Dryden Press, 1977.

Lewty, Marjorie. "An Author's Own Story," *Harlequin* III No. 10, pp. 68-70.

Logan, Joe. "Rhapsody in purple prose, all for 99 cents," *Minneapolis Star*, September 25, 1981, pp. 1B 4B.

Lopata, Helena Z. *Occupation: Housewife*. London: Oxford University Press, 1971.

Mann, Dr. Peter H. *A New Survey: The Facts About Romantic Fiction*. London: Mills and Boon, 1974.

Maryles, Daisy. "Harlequin to Launch Mystique Books Via Tested Market Strategies," *Publishers Weekly* 214 (August 28, 1978), pp. 375-76.

— "Some Facts and Figures." *Publishers Weekly* 220 (November 13, 1981), p. 26.

— and Robert Dahlin. "Romance Fiction," *Publishers Weekly* 220 (November 13, 1981), p. 25.

Mayer, Jean. *Overweight: Causes, Cost and Control*. New York: Prentice-Hall, 1968.

Meisler, Stanley. "'Soap'-style market plan aids Harlequin," *Minneapolis Star*, November 28, 1980, p. 1D.

Millman, Marcia. *Such a Pretty Face*. New York: W.W. Norton and Co., 1980.

Modleski, Tania. *Loving With a Vengeance: Mass-Produced Fantasies for Women*. Hamden, Connecticut: Archon Books, 1982.

Morgan, Alice. *The Sands of Malibu*. New York: Dell, 1982.

Mussell, Kay J. "Beautiful and Damned: The Sexual Woman in Gothic Fiction," *Journal of Popular Culture* IX (Summer 1975), pp. 84-89.

Nelson, Martha. "Sweet Bondage: You and Your Romance Habit," *Ms* XI No. 8 (February 1983), pp. 97-98.

New York Times, "Expanding Romance Market," March 8, 1982, pp. 21, 24.

Novik, Mary. "A Harlequin Serenade," *Books in Canada* 7, No. 9 (November 1978), pp. 4-7.

Oakley, Ann. *The Sociology of Housework*. New York: Pantheon Books, 1974.

Ontario Public Interest Research Group. *Reed International: profile of a transnational corporation*. Toronto: OPIRG Inc., 1977.

O'Toole, Patricia. "Paperback Virgins," *Human Behavior* 8 (February 1979), pp. 63-67.

Parkin, Frank. *Class Inequality and Political Order*. London: Paladin, 1972.

Patterson, Janet. "Consuming Passion," *Fireweed* 11 (1981), pp. 19-33.

Pendleton, Don. *Return to Vietnam*. Toronto: Worldwide, 1982.

Peplau, L.A., A. Rubin and C.T. Hill. "Sexual intimacy in dating relationships," *Journal of Social Issues* 33, No. 2 (1977), pp. 86-109.

Perebinossoff, Philippe. "What Does a Kiss Mean? The Love Comic Formula and the Creation of the Ideal Teenage Girl," *Journal of Popular Culture* VIII (Spring 1975) pp. 825-35.

Perun, Halyna. "Harlequin lays off 85 workers in bid to halt profits' plunge," *Globe and Mail,* September 17, 1983.

Publishers Weekly. "Harlequin Launches Million-Dollar T V Campaign in U S Market," CCVIII (September 29, 1975), pp. 38, 40.

Raab, Jamie. "Romance on the Job," *Romantic Times* 6 (Summer 1982), p. 21.

Ray, Lovelle. "The American Woman in Mass Media: How Much Emancipation and What Does It Mean?" *Toward a Sociology of Women,* ed. Constantina Safilios-Rothschild. Toronto: Xerox Publishing, 1972, pp. 41-62.

Redekop, Donald. "For This Publisher, Books are a Product to be Sold as if They Were Candy Bars," *Financial Post,* August 9, 1975, p. C8.

Reed, J.D. "From Bedroom to Boardroom," *Time,* April 13, 1981, pp. 101-102.

Rich, Adrienne. "Compulsory Heterosexuality and Lesbian Existence," *Powers of Desire: The Politics of Sexuality,* eds. Ann Snitow, Christine Stancell and Sharon Thompson. New York: Monthly Review Press, 1983.

Richardson, Dorothy. "The Long Day: The Story of a New York Working Girl," *Women at Work,* ed. William L. O'Neill. Chicago: Quadrangle Books, 1972.

Robertson, Ian. *Sociology*. New York: Worth Publishers, 1977.

Romantic Times, "News Flash!" *RT7* (Fall 1982), p. 9.

Royster, Vermont. "The Reading Addiction," *The Wall Street Journal,* June 24, 1981, p. 20.

Rubin, Lillian B. *Intimate Strangers: Men and Women Together*. New York: Harper and Row, 1983.

— *Worlds of Pain: Life in the Working-Class Family.* New York: Basic Books, 1976.

Rudolph, Barbara. "Heartbreak comes to Harlequin," *Forbes,* March 29, 1982, pp. 50-51.

Russ, Joanna. "Somebody's Trying to Kill Me and I Think It's My Husband," *Journal of Popular Culture* VI (Spring 1973), pp. 666-91.

Safilios-Rothschild, Constantina. *Love, Sex, and Sex Roles.* Englewood Cliffs, New Jersey: Prentice-Hall, 1977.

Scully, C. Sue. "Harlequin Enterprises Ltd." *Midland Doherty Limited Newsletter,* May 1979, n.p.

Sherfey, Mary Jane. *The Nature and Evolution of Female Sexuality.* New York: Vintage Books, 1973.

Showalter, Elaine. *A Literature of Their Own: British Women Novelists From Bronte to Lessing.* Princeton, New Jersey: Princeton University Press, 1977.

Simon, Rita. *Women and Crime.* Lexington, Massachusetts: D.C. Heath, 1975.

Singer, Jerome L. *The Inner World of Daydreaming.* New York: Harper Colophon Books, 1975.

Small, Beatrice W. "What Is Romance Fiction?" *Publishers Weekly* 220 (November 13, 1981), pp. 26, 28-29.

Smith, Dorothy. "An Analysis of Ideological Structures and How Women Are Excluded," *The Canadian Review of Sociology and Anthropology* XII No. 4 Part 1 (November 1975), pp. 353-69.

Smith, Wendy. "An Earlier Start on Romance," *Publishers Weekly* 220 (November 13, 1981), pp. 56, 58, 60-61.

Snitow, Ann. "Mass Market Romance: Pornography for Women is Different," *Radical History Review* 20 (Spring/Summer 1979), pp. 141-61.

Sonenschein, David. "Love and Sex in the Romance Magazines," *Side Saddle on the Golden Calf* ed. George H. Lewis. Palisades, California: Goodyear, 1972.

Stricker, Jeff. "Romance Novels Make Publishers Passionate About Sales," *Minneapolis Tribune,* December 18, 1981, pp. 1C, 4C.

Tennov, Dorothy. *Love and Limerence: The Experience of Being in Love.* New York: Stein and Day, 1979.

Thurston, Carol. "The Liberation of Pulp Romances," *Psychology Today* April 1983, pp. 14-15.

Toth, Emily. "Who'll Take Romance?" *The Women's Review of Books* Vol. 1 No. 5 (February 1984), pp. 12-13.

Turner, Alice K. "The Romance of Harlequin Enterprises," *Publishers Weekly* CCIV (September 3, 1973), pp. 31-32.

Valentina. "Under the Covers," *Romantic Times* 6 (Summer 1982), p. 4.

Watt, Ian. *The Rise of the Novel.* Harmondsworth, Middlesex, England: Penguin Books, 1957.

Weinberger, David. "The Case of Yellow Fever," *Macleans* 94 (September 14, 1981), pp. 72, 74, 76.

Westell, Dan. "Torstar Bids for Harlequin," *Globe and Mail,* March 13, 1981, p. B1.

Willoughby, Jack. "Harlequin's Chief's Projections Show More Happy Endings On Movie Screen," *Globe and Mail,* July 16, 1977, p. B5.

Wilson, Diane. "Passion! Fury! The Battle for the romance novel market," *Canadian Business,* July 1980, pp. 24-25.

The Women's Bureau, Ontario Ministry of Labour. *Women in the Labour Force "Basic Facts."* Ontario: Ministry of Labour, Women's Bureau, undated.

HARLEQUINS CITED

Anderson, Jan. *Master of Koros,* 1974.
Ashton, Elizabeth. *My Lady Disdain,* 1976.
Bavling, Jayne. *Wait for the Storm,* 1982.
Brett, Rosalind. *Sweet Waters,* 1964.
— *Young Tracey,* 1964.
Britt, Katrina. *Flowers for My Love,* 1980.
Burchell, Mary. *Yours With Love,* 1981.
Carter, Rosemary. *Daredevil,* 1983.
Clair, Daphne. *The Loving Trap,* 1982.
Clifford, Kay. *No Time for Love,* 1982.
Cork, Dorothy. *A Promise to Keep,* 1974.
Corrie, Jane. *Rimmer's Way,* 1977.
Craven, Jane. *Dark Summer Dawn,* 1982.
Dingwell, Joyce. *Corporation Boss,* 1976.
— *Greenfinger's Farm,* 1966.
Donnelly, Jane. *Rocks Under Shining Water,* 1973.
Douglas, Sheila. *Return to Lanmore,* 1980.
Doyle, Amanda. *Play the Tune Softly,* 1967.
Ellis, Janine. *Rough Justice,* 1980.
Field, Sandra. *Walk by My Side,* 1983.
— *The Winds of Winter,* 1981.
Gillen, Lucy. *The Pretty Witch,* 1974.
Graham, Elizabeth. *Stormy Vigil,* 1982.
Hampson, Anne. *For Love of a Pagan,* 1979.
— *The Rebel Bride,* 1973.
— *South of the Moon,* 1979.
— *To Tame a Vixen,* 1979.
Harrel, Linda. *Sea Lightning,* 1980.
Henaghan, Rosalie. *Coppers Girl,* 1982.
Hilliard, Nerina. *Dark Star,* 1969.
Holland, Sarah. *The Devil's Mistress,* 1982.
Hoy, Elizabeth. *Into a Golden Land,* 1971.
Hunter, Elizabeth. *Spiced With Cloves,* 1966.
Jordan, Penny. *Marriage Without Love,* 1981.
Kidd, Flora. *Between Pride and Passion,* 1982.
— *Passionate Stranger,* 1981.
Lake, Patricia. *The Silver Casket,* 1983.
Lamb, Charlotte. *Desire,* 1981.
— *Midnight Lover,* 1982.
Lane, Roumelia. *Harbour of Deceit,* 1975.
Lewty, Marjorie. *The Short Engagement,* 1978.
Maclean, Jan. *An Island Loving,* 1982.
Malcolm, Margaret. *Little Savage,* 1968.

Mortimer, Carole. *Perfect Partner,* 1983.
— *Red Rose for Love,* 1982.
Nel, Stella Francis. *Golden Harvest,* 1973.
Nickson, Hilda. *The Man in Possession,* 1970.
Norrell, Marjorie. *Promise the Doctor,* 1966.
Pargeter, Margaret. *Not Far Enough,* 1982.
Seale, Sara. *Cloud Castle,* 1967.
Sellers, Alexandra. *Season of Storm,* 1983.
Shore, Juliet. *When Doctors Meet,* 1968.
Summers, Essie. *Through All the Years,* 1975.
Thorpe, Kay. *Rising Star,* 1969.
— *Temporary Marriage,* 1982.
Way, Margaret. *Broken Rhapsody,* 1982.
Weale, Anne. *Islands of Summer,* 1965.
— *A Touch of the Devil,* 1982.
Wentworth, Sally. *Flying High,* 1983.
— *The Judas Kiss,* 1982.
— *Liberated Lady,* 1979.
West, Nicola. *Lucifer's Brand,* 1983.
Whittal, Yvonne. *Chains of Gold,* 1983.
— *The Lion of LaRoche,* 1982.
Wibberley, Mary. *Dark Viking,* 1975.
Winspear, Violet. *Desert Doctor,* 1965.
— *The Man She Married,* 1983.
Wyndham, Esther. *Once You Have Found Him,* 1964.